# Toxic Stress

# Toxic Stress

A step-by-step guide to managing stress

## DR HARRY BARRY

*This book is dedicated to my mother, Dilly Barry (1922–2010)*

*'The butterfly has flown!'*

First published in 2010 by Liberties Press, Ireland
This revised and updated edition published in 2017 by Orion Spring,
an imprint of The Orion Publishing Group Ltd
Carmelite House, 50 Victoria Embankment
London EC4Y 0DZ

An Hachette UK Company

1 3 5 7 9 10 8 6 4 2

A CIP catalogue record for this book is
available from the British Library.

ISBN: 978 1 4091 7447 9

Typeset by Input Data Services Ltd, Somerset

Printed in Great Britain by CPI Group (UK) Ltd, Croydon, CR0 4YY

MIX
Paper from
responsible sources
FSC® C104740

www.orionbooks.co.uk

# A Note to Readers

This book was originally published in 2010 as part of the *Flag* Series. In preparation for the launch of the series in UK and abroad, I have taken the opportunity to refresh and update the whole series. I have updated therefore some parts of *Toxic Stress*, to include some new insights into this condition in what is an ever-changing field.

*Toxic Stress* is a handbook that will hopefully assist many in understanding and teasing out the main stress issues in their lives. Many will be able to apply the approaches discussed to their own situations and will need no further assistance. Some, however, may want to seek out a counsellor, CBT therapist or family doctor to travel with them on the journey back to mental health. I exhort you to do so if you feel that this will be of assistance. The old adage, 'a problem shared is a problem halved', still resonates!

Some of those who read this book may find themselves in a dark place. Some may feel hopeless or helpless, unable to see any future. Some may even be planning to end the pain and despair they feel. They may feel that they would be doing those close to them a 'favour' by ending their life or they may be too distressed even to consider the consequences for those left behind.

If you are in this state of mind, I exhort you to come forward and look for help. Men in particular find it very difficult to open up and talk about how they feel. The first step, of opening up to somebody you trust, is often extremely hard to do, but it is a crucial one for the journey back to mental health. If you are unable to do this, at the back of this book is a list of excellent groups with telephone numbers and website addresses. *Make that call*. Apart from changing your life, talking to someone may save those close to you from a lifetime of pain and suffering.

All the case histories and individual references in this book are allegorical in nature.

# CONTENTS

# INTRODUCTION

As modern life gets increasingly complex and the pace of life increases exponentially, stress is rapidly becoming almost endemic to our lives. We in Ireland and the UK, along with most of the developed world, have passed through two tumultuous decades. We initially went through a decade of extraordinary growth followed by the greatest financial crashes of the past hundred years. This has led to the rapid growth of toxic stress into our lives. When we add in the technological revolution and the growing influence of social media, it is no wonder that stress is a word constantly on our lips. Increasingly we can recognize just how 'stressed out' we are much of the time, but struggle as to how best to manage it.

The word 'stress' is one of the most commonly used and least understood buzzwords of modern life. Through researching conditions affecting mental health in my previous books, I have become increasingly convinced that unhealthy forms of stress are perhaps the greatest single threat to our physical and mental well-being. The purpose of this book is to explore this phenomenon in more detail.

I use the term 'toxic', as it adequately describes the harmful effects that stress can lead to. Stress can lead to a host of serious conditions, both physical and psychological. Such physical ailments include heart attacks, cancer, diabetes, strokes and infertility, while psychological effects of stress include depression and suicide.

There has recently been a stream of high-profile cases in the media, sport and business which have revealed the tragic consequences of toxic tress in the lives of well-known public figures. However, chronic stress can affect people

1

from all walks of life, and has become endemic in modern Ireland, the UK USA, Europe and elsewhere. Because many of us are unaware of the presence of chronic stress in our lives, or of just how damaging it can be, we fail to confront this silent menace.

This book can best be described as a step-by-step 'stressbuster' guide and one that will hopefully reshape and improve the lives of many of its readers!

The first part of this book will lay the groundwork for the rest of the book. It aims to define what stress is, and how it can take on unhealthy aspects. I will explain the evolutionary origins of stress, the impact it has on our bodies and brain, and the fact that our behavioural response to it can be as damaging as the stress itself. I will also explain why some of us are more vulnerable to stress and its effects than others, the different ways in which men and women's bodies handle stress, and will also argue that it is crucially important to teach children skills to help them cope with stress from an early age. We will also be examining the role of technology in creating much of the stress we are now experiencing and also the impact of an increasingly unstable world politically and security-wise on our stress system.

The first section will deal with the positive nature of stress and why this is also important in our lives. But it will also deal with the significant impact that toxic stress can have on our mental health and how it can lead to increased anxiety, depression and self-harm.

In the second part of the book, I will present a seven-step programme which is designed to help identify unhealthy stress in our lives. This programme includes methods that can be used to 'detoxify' stress, in particular changes in thinking and behaviour. I will put forward numerous case studies involving highly stressful situations in everyday life, and show how the people involved learned to reduce their levels of harmful stress to a healthier level.

Readers may notice a strong emphasis in this book on the links between stress and suicide; I make no excuses for placing this issue squarely in the centre of the discussion. We are in the middle of a crisis in Ireland, not in economic terms, as thankfully the recession is over and unemployment is now down to pre-recession terms; but in terms of the loss of hundreds of young and not so young lives due to suicide. The greater the stress being put on our young men in particular, the more likely it is that depression, self-harm and death by suicide will emerge, resulting in lifetimes of sadness and guilt for those left behind.

Learning to identify and cope with toxic stress can lead to a happier and more contented life, reduce the risks of a host of physical illnesses like heart attacks, strokes and cancer, decrease our risks of anxiety and depression and in some cases, save lives by lessening the curse of young male suicide affecting Ireland, the UK and many other parts of the developed world.

# PART ONE

Experts in the field of stress define the phenomenon in a different way to the layperson. To the latter, anything they find difficult in their lives is described as stressful, but stress itself is poorly understood. Even within the fields of science and medicine, there exist numerous definitions of stress, depending on the perspective being taken. It is unsurprising, therefore, that the term is so often misused.

The key difficulty is that we usually don't separate the cause of our stress (the *stressor*) from the activation of our body's stress system (the *stress response*). Stress refers to the latter, so it can be defined as 'the reaction of our stress system to an internal or external stressor'. This is an important distinction, as it implies that stress can be healthy or unhealthy, depending on how the stress system responds to a particular situation.

In practice, most people use the term 'stress' in a purely negative sense, to describe situations where a particular stressor renders them unable to cope, leading to a host of negative physical and mental symptoms. This experience is referred to *by us all* as 'being stressed'.

A simple example would be Jim, who is going to attend a job interview in a few hours time. He feels edgy, his muscles are tense, and his stomach is in knots. While Jim finds these sensations uncomfortable, they are not unhealthy. In this case, the stress response is a natural reaction to the upcoming interview, and its purpose is to help Jim perform to an optimal level.

This type of stress is short-term, or 'acute', and is generally not harmful. Stress can be acute or chronic, healthy or unhealthy, depending on both the length of time for which we experience it and its effects on our physical and mental well-being. Usually, toxic stress occurs when our stress response is chronic and unhealthy. Our mental interpretation of a stressor is just as important as the stressor itself. In the example above, Jim's interpretation that he will not be sufficiently prepared for his interview is leading him into as much trouble as the interview itself.

# 1. OUR STRESS SYSTEM

Throughout human evolution, survival has been the highest priority. As threats to that survival were mainly physical ones, we developed fast responses and reactions to deal with dangers in our environment. The whole body had to be able to gear up instantly to face such threats, and our internal stress system developed to cope with these demands. Our stress system needed to remain on high alert until such threats had passed. This system would switch off when it was not needed, during periods of inactivity or relaxation.

Three different situations could trigger the stress response in our ancestors. First, one needed to fight to defend against a threat to oneself or one's family. Secondly, where fighting would be unlikely to be successful, one would flee to ensure survival. In the third case, where life was in danger for a longer period of time, through food scarcity or sustained attack from enemies, the stress system would need to remain constantly active. In each scenario, the stress system would help facilitate the appropriate response until one was no longer in danger and survival was assured. This response was controlled by the brain, which chose to switch the stress response on or off depending on what was happening in the environment

Even though most of us no longer encounter such life-threatening situations in our daily lives, the structure, function and organisation of the stress system has changed little from the early period of human evolution. What *has* changed, however, is the nature of the stressors that exist today. While we don't face such acute and obvious dangers as our ancestors did, the challenges presented to us today are less clear-cut, making it difficult for the body to react with an appropriate stress response, resulting in a prolonged activation of our stress system. The stress response was only ever intended as a short-term emergency state of increased alertness, whereas the stress people experience today is long-lasting. Our bodies did not evolve to cope with such chronic stress, and it poses serious risks to our health. In short, the stress system that ensured the survival of our ancestors is threatening our lives today.

Another important difference between the stress experienced by our ancestors and stress as we know it today is the way in which we cope with it. In ancient times, human beings were generally fit and active, and this helped 'burn off' symptoms of stress. In modern times, however, many of us do not exercise, and our response to stress is often to over-eat, drink alcohol and smoke cigarettes – all of which are detrimental to our physical and mental well-being.

To understand why unnecessary and prolonged activation of the stress system can lead to long-term unhealthy effects, we first need to examine the stress system itself.

## The Brain's Response to Stress

The prefrontal cortex, or the 'logical brain', is located at the front of our brain; in the middle of our brain sits the limbic system, or 'emotional brain'.

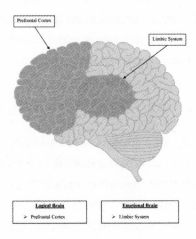

*Figure 1: The logical brain and the emotional brain*

Our behaviour is heavily influenced by the flow of information between these two areas. The part of the brain which controls our stress system is called the amygdala, or 'stress box', and is part of the emotional brain.

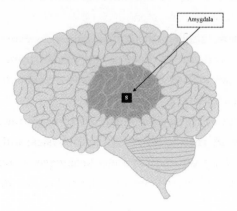

*Figure 2: The stress box*

When under attack from an internal or external stressor, the stress box is able to activate the body's physical response. Our ultimate response to a stressor, however, will be determined by the interaction between our logical and emotional brain. If the stress system is activated, the stress box releases small messengers within the brain that result in both nervous-system and hormonal responses. I will now look at these responses in more detail, and give three everyday examples to demonstrate how they work.

## The Nervous System Response

This response involves the activation of a system of nerves which reach almost every organ in the body, called the *autonomic nervous system* (ANS). This system is essential for our survival, as organs such as the heart, lungs and gut are being constantly monitored and activated by it. The system consists of two components, both of which play a major role in the stress response. The first of these is the *sympathetic nervous system* (SNS); its function is to 'hype up' the body in order to cope with stressors. Its activation is responsible for our acute symptoms of stress: it prompts a faster heartbeat, dry mouth, an unsettled feeling in the gut, dilated pupils and sweating. The system prepares our body to 'fight or flee' in response to a threat by temporarily diverting energy away from non-essential functions such as digestion, and towards the muscles, heart and lungs.

The second system is called the *parasympathetic nervous system* (PNS); its function is to calm us down when we are not under stress. It slows the heartbeat to a normal pace, allows digestion of food, and relaxes our muscles: the 'rest and digest' functions.

The response of the SNS to stress is straightforward: the nerves directly activate all organs which may be able to assist in dealing with the stressor. This system also leads to the activation of a secondary hormonal response.

## The Hormonal Response

This is activated by the brain when the stress box sends messengers to the hypothalamus/pituitary gland, or 'hormone control box'.

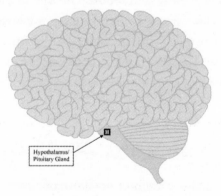

Hypothalamus/
Pituitary Gland

*Figure 3: The hormone control box*

This in turn sends hormones into the bloodstream and on to the adrenal glands, which sit on top of the kidneys. The adrenal glands are at the heart of our stress response. Each adrenal gland consists of a central core called the adrenal medulla and an outer shell called the adrenal cortex. The adrenal medulla produces our two acute stress hormones, adrenalin and noradrenalin, and is activated by the SNS. The adrenal cortex, by contrast, is strongly activated by hormones sent from the brain and produces the chronic stress hormone glucocortisol.

These stress hormones are then released into the bloodstream and travel around the body to further activate organs involved in the stress response, such as the heart, lungs and gut. Each of the stress hormones plays a different role in the stress response.

**Adrenalin** is released when we encounter an acutely stressful situation where we feel fear and our natural response is to flee. An example would be where we are confronted with someone wielding a knife and demanding our wallet! Adrenalin is also the hormone released during a panic attack. This is the hormone that causes us to feel a sense of dread and a strong drive to 'do a runner' when we sense a danger of any form.

**Noradrenalin** is released when we encounter an acutely stressful situation where our feeling is anger and our response is aggression. *So, noradrenalin is often called our aggression hormone!* An example would be where we may try to wrestle the knife from our attempted mugger! How we handle acute stress – whether we fight or flee – depends on the relative amount of adrenalin or noradrenalin released into our system.

**Glucocortisol** is released when we encounter a stressful situation that persists for a long period of time. Its function is to provide the energy required to keep the stress response active as long as it is needed. As we will see later, the production of consistently high levels of this hormone over an extended period of time results in many of the serious consequences of toxic stress. *It is often called our chronic stress hormone!*

To summarise, when we encounter acute stress, the brain decides on the appropriate response through interaction between its logical and emotional areas. The stress box *(amygdala)* is activated, and this switches on the SNS. If the response is to flee, the SNS instructs the adrenal gland to produce adrenalin, and we prepare to run, with fear being the emotion experienced. If the response is to fight, the adrenal gland releases noradrenalin, with the emotion experienced being anger. If the stress becomes chronic, the stress box sends information through the hormone control box, instructing the adrenal gland to produce glucocortisol to prolong the stress response. The role of our PNS is to allow the stress system to take a breather and encourage the body to relax. Without the PNS, we would live in such a state of acute stress that we would quickly burn out. For those who are interested in meditation it is the PNS that creates the feelings of calm and relaxation during this exercise.

Here are three examples of our stress system in action.

## Example 1

Mary is returning home late at night. She is close to home when she notices a man hanging around across the road. He has a hood up over his head and appears to be watching her intently. Her logical and emotional brains go into overdrive. She feels afraid, and experiences an instinctive desire to run the last few yards to her front door. Her SNS is activated, which encourages the adrenal gland to pour out adrenalin into her bloodstream. Her heart rate soars, her breathing becomes shallower, her pupils dilate, she begins to sweat, and her stomach clenches tightly. All of these things prepare her to bolt to her front door – which she succeeds in doing. On entering her house, she meets her brother and begins to relax, until eventually her adrenalin levels return to normal. In this situation, her natural stress reaction has potentially saved her from danger.

## Example 2

Dave is coming home with his girlfriend when he encounters an aggressive youth who threatens them both. As he feels he must protect his girlfriend, his stress system is activated in a different manner to Mary's in the previous example. His logical and emotional brains decide on an action other than fleeing. He experiences anger, and his stress box activates the SNS, which in turn releases noradrenalin into the bloodstream. His senses are heightened, his face displays aggression, his heart rate rises, his muscles tense, and he is poised to strike his assailant. He fends off the threat until his attacker flees. His acute stress response in this situation allows him to neutralise a threat to himself and his girlfriend.

## Example 3

Peter is called in to see his boss, who explains that the financial situation in the company is very challenging and that he cannot guarantee that Peter's job will be there by the new year, which is only four months away. When Peter hears the news, his stress system starts to pour out adrenalin due to the shock, and he feels fearful. As time goes by, his stress system begins to produce large amounts of glucocortisol. He starts to suffer from fatigue, broken sleep and poor concentration. He loses interest and enjoyment in life and feels constantly on edge, tense and worried. He describes the way he feels to his wife as 'tired but wired'. He suffers from cold sores and chest infections. He turns to alcohol to cope, but this only makes matters worse. He starts to feel down. All of these symptoms are indicators of chronic stress and are attributable to the persistently high levels of glucocortisol present in his system. Fortunately, when the new year arrives, his boss calls him in to tell him that his job is secure. After a few days, his stress system calms down, his glucocortisol levels finally wane, and his physical and mental health begin to recover.

In the first two examples, acute stress enabled the individuals to deal with threats. However, as can be seen in the third example, when the stress response becomes excessive and prolonged, we become unable to cope with the physical and mental demands that are placed on us. This is when stress becomes unhealthy, or toxic. The next section will examine the biological and behavioural consequences that result from this type of stress.

Let's start by examining the possible negative effects of the individual stress hormones.

## Noradrenalin

Of the two acute stress hormones, this is the one which is of most concern. It is released when our reaction to stress is either anger or frustration. Some people always respond to stress in this way. This hormone poses a number of potentially dangerous consequences to our vascular system, including:

- heart attacks in those with known or unidentified coronary heart disease
- serious electrical disturbances within the heart (arrhythmias), which can lead to sudden death
- a rise in blood cholesterol, increasing the risk of angina and heart attacks
- a rise in blood pressure, which is a risk factor in stroke and angina
- alterations in blood circulation in arteries leading to the brain, also increasing the risk of stroke

Individuals who continuously respond to stress with anger and frustration are therefore more likely to put their health at risk. For this at-risk group, reducing the risk of vascular incidents will involve retraining their response to stress. We can immediately see how important it is to recognize that dealing with stressful situations through anger or deep-seated frustration can put us at risk physically.

## Adrenalin

This hormone is released when our stress response is fear or anxiety. Although the symptoms associated with an excessive release of adrenalin are extremely unpleasant, they are not dangerous unlike those associated with noradrenalin.

Again for those who are reading this who suffer from panic attacks – this is the hormone that is producing all of the physical symptoms we experience. For those who would like to learn how to banish them from their lives please refer to *Anxiety and Panic* – another book in The Flag series!

## Glucocortisol

This hormone is released in large amounts in chronic stress, and is responsible for the mental and physical symptoms which appear when stress becomes toxic. A large volume of research has built up to show that this is harmful to both our body and mind in the following ways:

- increased blood sugar and diabetes
- increased cholesterol and triglycerides (blood fats), which increase the risk of heart attack and stroke
- higher levels of blood platelets, increasing the risk of heart attack and stroke
- damage to white blood cells, leading to viral and bacterial infections and reducing the body's ability to detect and destroy cancer cells, which are constantly being produced within the body
- shedding of calcium in bones, resulting in a risk of developing osteoporosis (thinning of the bones)
- increased sensitivity to pain due to a depletion of endorphins in the brain
- unhealthy weight loss or gain, depending on how the stress response affects appetite
- insomnia and resulting fatigue
- decreased libido and decreased fertility in men and women

The effects of high levels of glucocortisol on the immune system are worth examining in more detail. The natural pattern is higher levels of glucocortisol during the daytime and lower levels at night, but this is disrupted at times of chronic stress. During the day, our immune system tends to neutralise viruses and bacteria, and at night it helps destroy cancer cells. Consistently high levels of glucocortisol for a prolonged period of time disrupt these functions, making us prone to infections and less efficient in destroying cancer cells.

The main psychological consequences of chronically high levels of glucocortisol are as follows:

- mental fatigue (often misdiagnosed as physical fatigue)
- anxiety is common in the beginning of chronic stress, eventually leading to apathy
- damage to the mood system, which can trigger bouts of depression. High levels of glucocortisol during a person's childhood may damage key brain pathways, predisposing them to depression in later life. (For more on this, see *Flagging the Therapy* and *Depression*.)

- increased risk of suicide
- reduced capacity for enjoying life
- unhealthy behavioural responses, which exacerbate the problem

Most of the harmful effects of acute stress can be attributed to noradrenalin, and these effects are usually experienced by individuals who respond to stress with anger. However, it is important to note that this group can also succumb to the effects of glucocortisol if the stress becomes prolonged. It is clear from the above list that stress can be highly damaging to both body and mind, and potentially fatal.

Our behaviour in response to stress is of the utmost importance and will ultimately influence how stress affects our health. Unfortunately, often our natural response to persistent stress is to involve ourselves in a range of negative behaviours. Here are some of the more common and destructive ones:

- Smokers increasing the amount of cigarettes smoked per day, which further increases the risk of heart attack, stroke and lung cancer
- Serious misuse and abuse of alcohol to numb the physical and psychological symptoms of stress. This increases the risk of depression, suicide, addiction, liver disease and mouth cancer
- Avoiding exercise due to physical and mental fatigue, leading to obesity
- Changes in eating habits, with a risk of developing anorexia or obesity When obesity is combined with high levels of glucocortisol, diabetes can follow. Eating highly processed foods because we don't have the energy to cook properly increases our risk of bowel cancer
- Drinking caffeine, Coke or energy drinks to try and relieve fatigue, which increases the risks of anxiety, obesity and diabetes
- Some will respond with aggressive behaviour, such as road rage or fighting following an alcohol binge. This may lead to serious injury and impulsive violent acts towards themselves or others
- Some may turn to illegal drugs such as cocaine or hash to cope with persistent stress, despite the obvious dangers associated with these substances.

Others may begin to misuse prescription drugs, such as tranquillizers, and become addicted to them

As we can see, when the stress response is inappropriate, it can lead to a range of behaviours which threaten our physical and psychological well-being.

The brain is highly plastic and adaptable; prolonged exposure to persistent toxic levels of stress leads the brain to amplify our stress response so that we begin to live in a constant state of hyper-vigilance. This results in an over-production of noradrenalin and glucocortisol in particular – and all the risks that this entails. To reverse this process, we must encourage the brain to 'turn down the volume'!

Toxic stress can also be triggered by boredom or inactivity. In my line of work, I see many men suffering heart attacks or cancers shortly after retiring. I feel that it is their inability to adapt to their new lifestyle that is triggering such illnesses. It is possible that high levels of glucocortisol underlie these health problems.

The brain is the boss of our stress system and is responsible for analysing the stressors in our lives. If we expose the brain to persistently high levels of unhealthy stress, it will 'reset the system' and result in chronic stress.

However, the brain can be encouraged to revert back to normal. It is the plastic, or changeable, nature of the brain which helps us deal with toxic stress.

# 2. THE ANATOMY OF TOXIC STRESS

Now that we have an understanding of our stress response, and in particular how 'toxic stress' can be so damaging to our physical and mental health, let's turn our attention to the mechanisms which underlie the stress response. For stress to become harmful, four conditions are necessary:

- The stressor involved must be significant to us
- This stressor must be either chronic (present for a significant period of time) or involve regular periods of significant acute, severe stress to become a problem. This usually happens because we are unable to deal with the stressor
- It must overpower our innate resilience to stress, triggering the cascade of physical and psychological consequences already discussed
- It must be accompanied by unhealthy behaviour patterns that worsen the problem.

Let's take another example. John has worked in a company for many years and is quite happy with his job. A new manager is appointed; he wants to completely revamp the workplace.

John struggles with the changes and starts to interpret the situation incorrectly, believing that the manager does not like him and is trying to make his situation untenable in order to be able to let him go. Although this is not the case, it is John's perception of the situation.

Over time, John develops all the symptoms of chronic stress. He becomes increasingly exhausted, anxious, less efficient at work and snappy at home. He loses his usual sense of enjoyment of life and finally becomes apathetic. He starts to drink more at night and stops enjoying food and sex. In particular, he stops doing the one activity that might have helped him deal with his stress: taking exercise. Before his problems began, he had always taken a daily walk, but this fell by the wayside. He finally comes down with a bad viral illness as his immune system becomes compromised. He ends up spending a full month out of work on sick leave. It takes the combined efforts of his GP and a work-based counsellor to get him back on track.

How we view stressors depends on the 'lens' through which we have learned to view life. In the example above, the stressor involved was John's incorrect assumptions about the motives behind his manager's actions. Because he held these assumptions for some time, the stress response began to overpower John's natural resilience, and he moved into the world of toxic stress. We also see how his unhealthy behaviours of drinking, not exercising and eating poorly, together with the chronic stress response itself, led to him developing a viral illness and spending a month out of work.

Let's examine the four conditions necessary for toxic stress in more detail.

## The Stressor (or Our Interpretation of It) Must Be of a Significant Nature

All of us can easily identify many of the major stressors that can occur in our lives. We live in a fast-moving, technologically driven culture where the speed of change over the past decade has been staggering. Our society has been torn apart by the breakdown of traditional and community structures for a variety of social, economic, religious and political reasons. This has resulted in major stressors, some of the most common of which are listed below.

Relationship difficulties are a major source of acute and chronic stress. While separations and divorces are obvious stressors, even simple disagreements between couples can cause tremendous stress for those involved. Family conflicts can also be very stressful, and in many cases may last for years. It would be my own opinion after decades of helping people that relationship difficulties are one of the most powerful triggers for toxic stress.

It is worth also pointing out that many young adolescents are finding themselves in increasingly complex relationships and become extremely distressed when, as is often the case with life, things are not going their way. This can lead to long periods of chronic stress.

This situation is being complicated further by the cynical world of social media. We will be examining later the difficulties that social media creates for this group and indeed for us all, with significant impact on our mental health.

Exam pressures are another potent cause of chronic stress. This is largely attributable to the expectations heaped upon students by well-meaning parents, as well as the expectations of the student themselves. This stressor can potentially increase the risks of toxic stress, misuse of alcohol, depression, anxiety and self-harm.

We also see the college years as being a period when many young people become increasingly distressed. This is a period when many students struggle with toxic stress due to uncertainty about suitability of courses, living away from home for first time, financial pressures, coming to terms with being a young adult and many other stressors.

Loss – particularly the death of someone close to us – is a very powerful stressor and in some cases can have serious physical and psychological consequences. There are some types of loss that put an especially heavy load on our shoulders. Parents who lose a son or daughter to suicide can struggle with subsequent toxic stress for years often up to a decade later. Others who have lost much loved long-term partners or who have lost family members to trauma or cancer at an early age can also be extremely stressed as they struggle to cope with their overwhelming sense of loss. Grief can also result from the loss of a pet or the ending of a relationship.

Work pressures are another major stressor. Bullying in the workplace is one of the most insidious and potentially toxic causes of significant stress. What makes this stressor so toxic is the feeling that the victim has of being trapped with nowhere to turn. This can quickly eat away at our natural inner reserves and lead to long periods of intense prolonged chronic stress which can be so toxic to their physical and mental health. Nowadays, the fear of losing one's job is causing untold damage to the stress systems of many people. For some people, as we will see later, such fears of losing one's job produces typical adrenalin 'fear responses', and for others noradrenalin 'anger/frustration responses'.

A period of unemployment is a highly stressful time for many people – particularly if the person is experiencing it for the first time. Unemployment can lead to a significant loss in self-esteem and can generate huge financial pressure, which many people are simply unable to cope with.

Financial difficulties are another significant source of acute and chronic bouts of stress.

Debt and difficulties with banks, finance companies and moneylenders are particularly stressful. If these difficulties persist, they can threaten to overcome our stress system, sometimes with very serious consequences. We only have to look at our suicide rates and to see the consequences of this stressor.

Housing issues are another common stressor. These stressors, from challenges relating to building or extending a home to struggling to make mortgage repayments and dealing with negative equity and repossession, are likely to remain for decades.

Addiction is another stressor for both the addict and their family. Addiction is so destructive to a person's physical, psychological and social makeup that the stress response produced can be highly toxic.

The addict themselves often lives in a constant state of stress trying to feed their addiction and on occasions hide it from families and employers. They also commonly find themselves struggling with relationship and health difficulties created by their addiction. The consequences to their stress system can be devastating.

But it is often those living with the addict who suffer most. They live in a state of constant stress, wondering when the next bout of drinking or gambling or drug use is going to create havoc in their lives. They can live with financial difficulties related to the addict's behaviour and both spouses and offspring can be exposed on occasions to emotional and physical abuse. These can threaten to overpower their stress system.

Illness is highly stressful both for the sufferer and those close to them. Any significant illness challenges our internal stress system. Many result in physical and psychological symptoms and can present huge challenges for family members, as those who care for loved ones at home for long period can testify to. Some will succumb to toxic stress as a response.

Those who live with significant physical or mental handicap will be prone to stress, and those who look after them can also suffer from stress. Their situation is often quite like those who are looking after loved ones with dementia but their situation is often a lifelong commitment.

These are obvious significant stressors, but our interpretation of events can also result in toxic stress. Even though a stressor may seem relatively innocuous to others and actually present no real threat to us, it can still result in toxic stress. This may be the single most important factor when it comes to stress. Of all the disciplines, arguably CBT (cognitive behaviour therapy) has been most effective when it comes to dealing with this aspect of stress.

We now know that due to a combination of genetic and early environmental influences, each of us begins to develop internal belief systems through which we evaluate everything that happens to us from day to day. This plays a major role in deciding whether our primary emotional response to acute stress is fear, anger or frustration. This in turn can result in unhealthy behavioural responses.

I covered the 'ABC' system (practiced by CBT therapists and created by the psychotherapist Albert Ellis) in *Flagging the Therapy* and some of my other books and will be dealing with it in more detail later. But here is a summary of this system:

A Activating Event:
- Represents the stressor plus our interpretation of why it is bothering us.

B Beliefs:
- Represents our internal belief system/demands

C Consequences:
- Represents the emotional, physical and behavioural consequences which occur in response to a particular stressor.

To expand on this concept, we can say that our interpretation of the initial stressor is influenced by the underlying belief system we have developed (which usually involves making unrealistic demands on ourselves).

So if I begin to feel extremely stressed about any particular situation or event, analysing it using the 'ABC' system can often quickly reveal how I am feeling and why I am behaving as I am in response to it.

Let's take an example. Peter is becoming stressed. He feels he was passed over for promotion because he was not invited to apply for the post. In fact, his boss has been planning to transfer him to a different department as a promotion but does not want to reveal his hand yet. An 'ABC' analysis of the issue would go like this:

A   Peter does not get invited to apply for the position. He interprets this as a sign that he is not in favour with his boss and may be viewed as having few prospects with the company.
B   Peter looks for certainty that he will not be let go by the company.
C   Peter becomes highly stressed. He initially demonstrates an adrenalin fear/anxiety response but later becomes exhausted and stops sleeping, increases his alcohol intake and spends more and more time worrying about being let go.

In practice, it is Peter's erroneous interpretation of events, and his unrealistic demand that he must not be let go by his company, that is driving his toxic stress response. Crucially, it is often our incorrect analysis of events that triggers such responses. This will form an important component of how we deal with stress, as we will see.

## The Stressor Must Be Either Chronic (Present for a Significant Period of Time) or Involve Regular Periods of Severe, Acute Stress

As a general rule, stress only becomes toxic when we are exposed to persistent bouts of acute or chronic stress. An example of acute stress might be where we are intermittently exposed to episodes of bullying at work, and chronic stress might be where we lose our job and struggle to make ends meet over the subsequent year. Our stress system is usually quite robust and able to deal with less intense episodes of stress; exposure to significant or constant stressors puts us most at risk.

The stress system is engaged to deal with, and hopefully eliminate, the stressor. But as we all know, there are many situations in life where this is simply not possible, and so our stress system is forced to stay on high alert – with potentially dangerous results. Sometimes it is our own unhealthy belief system that may be driving the stress response: unless we get help to deal with this, the stress system will remain in overdrive.

A simple way of looking at the above is to regard our stress response as being controlled by a 'stress thermostat'. If we are exposed to long periods of persistent stress, the thermostat dial is set at a higher level – leading to toxic stress, and its consequences. Resetting the thermostat downwards will be one of the main planks of any successful approach to tackling the problem.

## The Stressor Must Overpower Our Innate Resilience to Stress

One of the most important concepts of mental health is that we are all different in the way we perceive and handle stress. We have known for decades that our genes and upbringing combine to create our individual, innate resilience to stress. In practice, this means that some of us cope better, both physically and mentally, with the 'slings and arrows' life throws at us. Genes like the 'Resilience Gene', which we will be discussing later play a key role in our potential vulnerability to stress. However, the environmental conditions pertaining to our development as babies, children, teenagers and young adults also play an important role in determining whether such genes are expressed.

Irrespective of our capacity to cope with stress, most of us, during certain periods of our lives, will feel that our world is 'falling in', and will end up battling the host of negative and unhealthy consequences which follow. For some of us, it may take major stressors to trigger such difficulties, but for others who are more vulnerable, relatively minor incidents may overwhelm our natural defences.

It must be emphasised that normal levels of stress are healthy and well tolerated by the brain and body. It is only when our response to a stressor is major and prolonged that our resilience may be overwhelmed. We will discuss this in more detail later.

## The Stressor Must Be Accompanied by Unhealthy Behaviours

For stress to be harmful, or toxic, associated unhealthy behavioural patterns are generally involved. This is because we struggle to deal with the negative mental and physical consequences of a stress response which has become prolonged, chronic and harmful to the body. In order to cope, we often turn to unhealthy behaviours such as smoking and alcohol misuse, and cease healthy behaviours such as eating properly and exercising.

# 3. STRESS: THE MODERN VIEW

Understanding the modern approach to stress requires knowledge of concepts such as:

- contentment and gratitude
- social support systems
- optimal stress levels
- lack of goals
- the importance of dignity

Contentment relates to the acceptance of oneself and one's life circumstances. There are likely to be situations where we lose our sense of contentment. This is often due to unrealistic expectations. Our expectations are often based on what we have learned when growing and developing as people, and may encourage us to build up mental pictures of where we 'should be', which are often different from where we actually are. Although we may feel that these aspirations are reasonable and achievable, they are often unrealistic and counterproductive. Sometimes we expect too much of ourselves, and demand too much from our situation. The more we demand such changes, the more stress we are likely to feel. By contrast, if we take a more pragmatic approach and accept that the world is unlikely to change to suit us any time soon, we are far less likely to experience the toxic effects of stress, and more likely to feel content with ourselves and our lives.

There is little doubt that the recent prolonged period of economic prosperity in Ireland and in many other developed countries threatened our sense of contentment due to its overemphasis on material possessions. The economic situation today challenges contentment for a markedly different reason: many of us are now struggling to make ends meet, or are adjusting to the fact of having a lower standard of living. There is a huge level of discontent amongst our current younger generations that this group might be the first ones to have to settle for a lower level of material and financial comfort than their parents. How we cope in either scenario depends on how comfortable we are with ourselves. If we expect too much of either ourselves or the situation we find ourselves in, we are likely to lose our sense of contentment and start to become stressed. A realistic appraisal of oneself and one's situation can greatly increase personal contentment and reduce the risk of chronic stress.

A close friend of contentment is gratitude and there is increasing interest in this positive emotion. One worries that many do not reflect on the positives they do have in life compared to many in deprived parts of the world whose struggle for survival is at a most basic level. Those of us fortunate enough to have worked in the developing world appreciate this perhaps the most. There will always be those who are less fortunate than ourselves and we do need to be grateful for all those little things in life which we so often take for granted – the commonest of these being the love of those who care for us!

There is little doubt that lack of contentment with our lives and an absence of gratitude for the good things we have in life are two powerful causes of toxic stress. In general, they are created more by our unrealistic demands and expectations. This is often where we must go to learn to deal with toxic stress.

Social support systems are a critical component in the battle against toxic stress. If we have supportive relationships, with both family members and partners, we are likely to deal with stressful situations far more successfully. Therefore, how we handle severe stress will in part depend on how stable our social relationship networks are. Social support systems seem to act as an emotional buffer zone between us and the stressor in question. While perhaps not eliminating the stress experienced, these relationships certainly help us cope with the stressor in question. This makes sense as people are not meant to be on their own, although for some this may be what life throws at them.

Having warm empathic relationships and friendships allow us to share the burdens of life and thus reduce our stress levels. In Ireland, we have a lovely old saying in Gaelic which translates into 'two shorten the road'. The thinking behind it is that as we are travelling on a journey just having someone there to chat away to and share the experiences on the way shortens and makes the trip more enjoyable. If we have on the journey of life such supportive relationships, they will genuinely reduce our risks of toxic stress arriving.

But we also need to examine the role of social support mechanisms at a community level. There has been a sea change in modern society. In former times the individual existed in a nuclear family but enveloped in the warm embrace of extended family and the local community.

Because of the complete splintering of both families and communities from a combination of economic difficulties, housing issues, emigration, couples often having to move far away from families and many other factors, these support systems are collapsing. In the past, children for example were often reared with the assistance of both grandparents and in a wider sense by the local community. To quote another old Irish saying – it takes a village to rear a child. Now there is an almost unhealthy reliance on the nuclear family itself to not only rear the child but to be able to be self-sustaining emotionally and practically in so many other ways.

These factors can lead to increased isolation for individuals and couples and a sharp resulting rise in stress levels as they attempt to navigate through the difficulties of life without these key support mechanisms in place.

There is also the increasing cult of the individual where previously more emphasis was put on the importance of the group or community. The more we begin to regard our own well-being as of more importance than those we share our world with, the more stressed we are doomed to become.

Increasingly I feel in decades to come we will come to recognize that one of the most powerful causes of toxic stress in our lives is this move from community support systems to increased reliance on the individual and the nuclear family.

Paradoxically, the very same social support systems if misused can move toxic stress moved away from the nuclear family and pass it on to grandparents.

The latter will always love being with their grandchildren but may on occasions be overwhelmed if asked to take over too much of the burden of rearing them. In the past, they too could have relied on the wider community to assist them in this process but now that option is no longer available to them. So many end up feeling incredibly stressed and yet also feeling guilty if they try to broach their difficulties to the parents of their grandchildren. This stress can on occasions become extremely toxic and lead to a lot of physical and psychological fallout.

Optimum stress level is an important concept when dealing with stress. The brain requires a certain minimum level of daily stress to function properly. Stress therapists feel that we need to raise our stress levels to a moderate level and try and keep them there. Too much or too little stress reduces our ability to cope with life. Keeping stress at an optimal level is a considerable challenge, but it is important for maintaining good mental health.

It is worth examining this concept in more detail. There has been an enormous amount of research done on the importance of keeping our stress system 'fine-tuned'. We discussed earlier the importance of our chronic stress hormone glucocortisol. If levels are too high as we discussed earlier then there can be a lot of significant physical and mental consequences. So clearly too much stress in our lives is not healthy.

But if we find that our lives are completely devoid of stress this can lead sometimes to the opposite situation occurring and we can become apathetic and become less capable of dealing with life's difficulties.

Neither situation is healthy and the ideal is where we feel a certain 'tension' in our everyday lives but not to a level where we feel we can no longer cope!

Lack of goals is a concept that refers to stress arising from a perceived lack of purpose in life. It is particularly relevant for work-related stress. People in their middle years have often achieved goals they set out for themselves in life but have not created any new ones. As a result, they may begin to feel useless. They may float along aimlessly, losing their sense of contentment and becoming stressed in response to even minor problems. Women and to a lesser extent men, when reaching their late forties and early fifties, may experience 'empty nest' syndrome. After devoting much time to their children and making considerable sacrifices, they feel that a huge gap is left when their offspring leave home. Many no longer feel useful and struggle to carve out a future role for themselves. Such disillusionment and discontent can result in toxic stress, and alcohol is often used as a coping mechanism.

Another at-risk group is those who retire – either due to age, redundancy or illness. These individuals may feel helpless, bored and apathetic. Having lost interest in life, they may become severely stressed. A commonly proposed solution to these scenarios is to set new goals or, as I would prefer to describe it, develop new passions.

Aimless 'floating' through life can be extremely destructive to our mental and physical health: we need to keep activating and challenging our minds to stay well. Passion for any activity or hobby 'switches on' our brain in a potent way, creating a protective environment that wards off toxic stress. If you find yourself 'floating' in this way, you need to recognise it and understand how damaging it can be to your mental and physical health. Then you need to open yourself to your inner passions and act on them. Many have developed a great sense of contentment upon discovering their creative skills and being courageous enough to embark on such a journey.

Using these concepts, we can learn new ways to find contentment in life, by setting realistic goals, discovering new interests, and keeping our stress levels at a constant but healthy level.

The importance of dignity is perhaps one of the least-discussed topics in understanding how we as human beings cope with stress. With the industrial/technological revolution of the past two hundred years, in many cases the place of the human being has been downgraded. We are often seen as mere 'economic units', of little worth in ourselves.

Thus, our job can often come to define who we are – and so, if we lose our job, we often lose ourselves! The shame associated with no longer being a functioning economic unit when we are without work can bring on very high levels of toxic stress. We forget that we are fathers, mothers, sons, daughters, neighbours and friends, and need to fully appreciate our importance to all of the people around us. Our real dignity lies not in what we 'do' but rather in who we are as people: special and unique. If we can introduce this concept into our daily lives, the protective effect is enormous.

## The Role of Genes and Upbringing in Toxic Stress

Why do some seem to handle stress much better than others and seem to suffer a lot from toxic stress?

Attention has shifted over and back as to whether this is due to genetic differences between those who seem to be more resilient to stress and those that are not and research into environmental effects as we are growing and developing on the same process.

Let's firstly examine the possibility that some are genetically hardwired to cope better than others with toxic stress in their lives.

One of the genes involved in predisposing us to toxic stress and indeed anxiety and depression is responsible for the manufacture and general levels of a key protein called the 'serotonin transporter' (the SERT molecule) which is a key player in our serotonin system in the brain (which is important for mood, sleep, sex, appetite and so on).

This little protein has been under observation for the past decade as a potential culprit in stress as well as anxiety/depression. The gene controlling the levels of this protein is passed on through generations. All of us have either short or long copies of this gene. It has been known for some time that those with two long copies are much more 'resilient' to stress than those with either one long and one short or, particularly, two short ones – who are much more likely to suffer from anxiety and, to a lesser extent, depression. We now know that those with small gene versions produce fewer SERT proteins. It now seems as if those with two short versions of this gene in particular have an amygdala or stress box in a constant state of hyper-vigilance, even when it is not being directly attacked by stress. Those with two long versions do not demonstrate this vulnerability. This led to the gene in question being called the Resilience

Gene. It is of course only one of a number of genes which may influence our capacity to handle stress.

But what about the place of environment as we are being reared? Does it play a role in whether such genes are switched on or off (a process called epigenetics)? Or do certain circumstances seem to predispose us from an early age to struggle with dealing with toxic stress?

One groundbreaking experiment by Michael Meaney (Professor of McGill University's Departments of Psychiatry, Neurology and Neurosurgery) gave us a unique insight into the answer to this question. He compared the stress response of rat pups whose mothers groomed them a lot in the first ten days of life versus those who did not. The former showed lower levels of our chronic stress hormone glucocorticoid and subsequently less anxiety and stress. The mechanisms involved were simple. Normally high glucocorticoid levels feed back to glucocorticoid receptors in the hypothalamus, reducing further production but, in the anxious rats, this feedback was ineffective. Further research showed that the receptor genes in the hypothalamus of the anxious rat pups showed many more methyl groups. These tended to switch off the genes in question, exaggerating the stress response, predisposing them to future toxic stress and anxiety for life.

There have been further research experiments, which have consolidated this insight. So it does seem as if both genes and our upbringing play an interactive role in deciding on whether we will handle toxic stress in our life well or really struggle.

# 4. STRESS AND THE DEVELOPING CHILD

One area increasingly coming under scrutiny is the role of stress in the developing child. For a child to develop normally, he or she needs to be somewhat exposed to the harsh realities of life, and to learn that life is not always fair, and that we cannot always have what we want. Parents sometimes try to shield their children from the difficulties of life: such overprotective behaviour puts the child at an increased risk of chronic stress when they are later exposed to life's challenges, as they will inevitably be. At the same time, exposing children to stress above and beyond what they can cope with will hype up their stress system, with long-term negative consequences. This is most often observed in children reared in abusive or addictive environments. The word 'resilience' is the term we use to describe our individual capacity to cope with stress. We now realize from research dealt with in my earlier books that children's brains are incredibly susceptible to stress during the key developmental stages from birth onwards. High glucocorticol levels can be very damaging to the immature developing brain. In extreme abuse situations children may end up with actual structural changes which predispose them to major depression later in life. We also know that some of those who lack resilience are far more likely to suffer from significant anxiety, will handle stress poorly as adults and are also unfortunately more at risk of self-harm.

There is widespread concern amongst many who work in education in that we are not getting this balance in parenting right and that many of our children and adolescents are suffering the consequences. There is an anxiety epidemic amongst our adolescent population and many educators and those who work in mental health that the source may lie in the inability of many of our young people to cope with stress. This is another way of saying that they are less resilient than in former times. I hope to deal with this whole area in a future book. But for now, suffice to say that we may find our future young adults more prone to the consequences of toxic stress in the future.

Parents are nowadays being bombarded with so much 'psychobabble' (some of which comes from pop psychology and some well-meaning advice from properly qualified experts) that it is proving difficult for them to trust their instinctive nature and allow the child to feel stress and discomfort in a monitored, healthy manner. We need to encourage resilience in young people, so that they can develop healthy stress systems to help them cope with the extremely complex world in which they find themselves.

# 5. TOXIC STRESS: THE ROLE OF PERSONALITY

The links between stress and personality have been under scrutiny for more than fifty years, with attempts to match particular personality types with harmful stress. But defining personality itself has proved difficult. The modern view is that, from a relatively early age, we all begin to exhibit particular *traits* which determine how we view things that occur in our lives – and that this in turn determines our behaviour. This behaviour is often regarded as the primary determinant of our personality type. We all develop our personality through a complex interaction between genes and our environment (*epigenetics*), which regulates the expression of these genes. Research into stress has identified four personality types:

TYPE A PERSONALITY is associated with those who are competitive, aggressive, impulsive, impatient and goal-orientated, and put themselves and those around them under considerable pressure to deliver targets. These people often take part in sports in order to achieve and may also engage in dangerous or unhealthy behaviours like driving aggressively, drinking and smoking. This aggressive, hostile behaviour is associated with an increased risk of developing coronary heart disease, due to the release of high levels of noradrenalin and glucocortisol and unhealthy behavioural patterns. Men seem to be more at risk of stress if they have this personality type – perhaps because they are more likely to be aggressive and angry in their behavioural responses to stress.

TYPE B PERSONALITY lies at the other end of the scale. It is associated with people who are less goal-orientated, calmer in response to problems, less aggressive and impulsive, and less likely to engage in the unhealthy behaviours described above. This group handles stress well and as a result are less inclined to suffer the symptoms of toxic stress.

TYPE C PERSONALITY is associated with people who are extremely passive and unassertive. They find it difficult to express their emotions, feelings or needs to others. People with type C personalities have been described as extremely cooperative, patient and accepting. They seldom display either anger or excitement and will rigidly control their facial expressions; they are usually highly introverted. These individuals suppress their feelings and do not stand up for themselves; as a result, they suffer more from stress and depression than any other personality type. Their immune system may end up attacking their own body. Their responses to stress also seem to increase their risk of developing and coping with certain types of cancer, such as malignant melanomas which grow on the skin (see Temoshok et al., 1987), and some forms of breast cancer, but the evidence for this is not completely conclusive! One of the functions of the immune system is to constantly monitor our body for cancer cells and kill them; perhaps the response of this group to stress may be compromising this process.

TYPE D PERSONALITY is associated with those who experience intense emotional distress, in social situations for example, but whose response is to lock it up inside themselves. They can be described as gloomy, anxious and socially inept. Type D behaviour is characterised by a tendency to avoid social contact with others. There is evidence that type D personality is associated with depressive and anxiety symptoms, post-traumatic stress disorder, social phobia and panic disorder. As is the case with type A personalities, when exposed to stress, this group is more at risk of heart disease due to the excessive release of noradrenalin and glucocortisol. High glucocortisol levels in particular predispose this group to an increased risk of heart disease.

Toxic stress is likely to be present where behaviour becomes extremely unhealthy. It is not any particular personality type which causes problems, but rather the person's response to stress which results in a predisposition to heart disease and cancer. Simply possessing some of the traits mentioned above does not necessarily mean that a particular person will experience significant risks to their health. Furthermore, other protective influences in our lives may shield us from these dangers. However, if any of the above personality trait descriptions seem to apply to you, it may be important for you to begin tackling stress.

Although personality itself is relatively stable over a person's life, it is possible to reshape patterns of thinking and behaviour and thus reduce the risk of toxic stress. Our brain has the capacity to change to facilitate this.

## Toxic Stress and the Role of Technology

When I was given the opportunity to update this book my most immediate concern was to address the links between toxic stress and technology, I have become as a mental health professional increasingly concerned about the effects the latter is having on our emotional and physical health. I also have grave concerns about us a society if we do not start examining this phenomenon. So, let's explore the issue further.

The arrival into our lives of both advancing technology interwoven with the insidious effects of social media invading every aspect of our being, has really turned up the thermostat of our stress system with the subsequent appearance often unnoticed of toxic stress into our lives.

Technology itself has been advancing at an exponential rate in the past ten to fifteen years. No sooner do we have the latest device than it seems as if it is already out of date. We are all becoming subtly drawn into a world where the machine is gradually taking over the simplest of tasks such as remembering basic information, counting without the need for a calculator, losing our ability to read maps and most worryingly of all, convincing us that real life is what happens through the medium of devices such as our smart phones and iPads rather than through face to face experiences with life.

But the issues run much deeper than this. We are becoming slaves to our machines, constantly on call to them twenty-four hours a day. The stress system is being constantly nudged into higher states of alertness with consequences we will examine later. This means that key players in our stress system such as the amygdala are being heated up, driving us closer and closer to toxic stress. The term we use for toxic stress – being 'tired but wired' takes on a new meaning when we realize that it is the smart phone for example in our pocket and constantly in our hands day and night that is wiring us up for future trouble.

I am constantly asked in large meetings as to why there is such an epidemic of stress and anxiety in our modern lives. My usual reply is to take out my smart phone and hold it up, explaining that this has been the real game-changer.

When computers arrived, we all thought that they and the internet would transform our lives and so they have. But it is hard to believe that the smart phone in your hand has more sophisticated technology in it than the most powerful computers used by security services in past few decades. It can do almost anything from instant access to emails, the internet, SMS messaging, taking of photos and videos to allowing us access to all forms of social media. And these are only some of the potential functions of these machines.

But this unbelievable machine is coming with a very high price tag and it is not a financial one. It should also be coming with a health warning – 'this device may be harmful to your physical and mental health by triggering toxic stress'! In practice, most would laugh at such a warning but in years to come I feel we may look back at this rather tongue in cheek observation and realise that it may be closer to the truth than we currently believe.

If we move on to add all forms of social media into the mix the risks increase further. At the heart of social media lies the extremely unhealthy belief that one human being can rate themselves and their lives against another. It has led to an obsession or preoccupation with physical appearances and the seeking of an unrealistic expectation of perfection in so many areas of our lives. Whilst there are clearly benefits to social media as with all modern technology, there are many pitfalls and the biggest is the constant pressure being exerted on our stress system to cope with the pressures of having the most perfect of lives and physical appearances. Never has this been more apparent than in the adolescent population. But it is acutely relevant to us all.

To try and explain just how stressful living with the combination of modern technology and social media combined can be, join me on a 'virtual tour' of a typical day in the life of a couple living in a major urban area or capital city such as London or Dublin or New York and see how their lives are being affected. They are just a microcosm of the way modern life is being overrun by the 'machine'. This is not to say that many of the issues we raise are not relevant to rural areas. It is just that they seem to be more obvious and perhaps more immediate in urban settings.

We will then examine how damaging technology and social media can be on our stress system based on what we will learn from this 'tour'.

## A Day in the Life of Philip and Anne

Philip comes awake at 5 am with the sound of his phone beeping yet again. He has resisted looking at it but he has become anxious that 'maybe there is something important he is missing'! He has tossed and turned during the night unaware that the blue light from both his partner's and his own phone is reducing his brain melatonin levels, making it harder for them to sleep.

He goes through the fifteen emails that have come in from different sources and then lies back down but struggles to fall back to sleep. His mind is already on high alert as to how best to deal with some of the issues raised in the emails. Meanwhile, his partner Anne has also been woken and almost without thinking is picking up her phone to check her Twitter account and emails. She too struggles to get back to sleep as she begins to worry about the upcoming day.

They both rise at 7 and try to wake their two adolescent children – Dan who is 13 and Lily who is 16. This proves to be extremely difficult as both had spent hours during the night on their smart phones, communicating with their peers on social media.

Eventually all four are at breakfast, which is a very silent affair. The TV is on with the latest bad news stories coming in through cable news. Lily has her earphones in, listening to music and checking her social media. Philip and Anne are frantically trying to eat whilst scrolling down through further emails and social media sites. Dan is slumped over his cereal as he is two or three hours sleep deprived.

Eventually, the children having been dispatched to school, Philip and Anne head off in different directions, one on the bus and the other on the tube. On the way, if they had been observant, they would have noticed how many people on the street had their earphones in, blocking out all sounds from the world, seemingly oblivious to others passing them by as they too kept checking their smart phones.

On the tube, if Philip had been more observant, he would have noticed that almost every single person was scrolling away, checking their social media sites, their likes and dislikes, the latest Twitter comments and, in the case of businessmen, their emails.

The main reason of course that Philip did not notice was that he too was doing the same. He did notice however that he was feeling very stressed – how was he going to be able to handle the avalanche of emails from work that would be awaiting him when he began his day. He had already dealt with twenty and this was only the start of the day.

Anne too was having a similar experience and was also feeling very fatigued. All around her, too, everybody was scrolling away, but she too did not notice, for she was reflecting on just how miserable she felt when she looked at the wonderful lives all her online friends seemed to be having. They all seemed to look much more attractive and their lives were so interesting. She noted how distant she and Philip had become and could not really understand why this would be so.

When both Philip and Anne arrive at their workplaces they head for the coffee machine to ward off the effects of fatigue and continue this pattern for the day. Neither has recognized that the reason for this fatigue is a combination of toxic stress and lack of sleep created by their interfacing with technology. Of course, coffee wires their stress system further, dehydrates them and leads to their mood and anxiety levels rising and falling during the day, not to mention Philip's frustration levels also rising!

Meanwhile the couple's two children were also busily using their smart phones. Lily was upset that her 'group' was ganging up online on her best friend. She was becoming increasingly stressed and anxious they would now turn on her. Dan was struggling with something different. His friends were busy watching porn online. He felt there was something wrong with him in that he felt uncomfortable with this. Maybe they would think he was gay. His stress levels began to rise uncontrollably.

All day, Philip and Anne were bombarded with all that technology and social media could throw at them. They both arrived home exhausted, irritable and feeling more and more stressed out. Their two children, as always, quickly retreated to their bedrooms, which were set out quite naturally like airline cockpit control centres! With music blaring through headphones, the computer on in one corner and their smart phones buzzing constantly – they tried to fit as much study as was possible into the time left when all social media commitments were over.

Philip just slumped into the armchair for the night and mindlessly watched TV whilst constantly checking his smart phones for emails. Anne was much more usefully employed checking out shopping sites and online social media sites. Finally, all take off to bed but make sure their smart phones are charging but right by their bedsides – to avoid missing anything during the night. They then struggle yet again to go to sleep – feeling tired but extremely wired. Till the following morning at 5 am when it all would begin again.

Whilst the above virtual tour reads like a George Orwell nightmare, it is a cameo of modern life. So, let's examine some of the issues apparent in this story and examine how they impact on our stress system to generate toxic stress.

If we start by looking at the whole area of sleep. The average adult requires between seven and eight hours of sleep per night for brain health. When we sleep, we both allow our brain to carry out essential repairs and also to reorganize our memories of the day which has passed. If anything disrupts our sleep patterns we become toxically stressed very quickly. If our brain is struggling with lack of sleep we become tense, anxious, depressed and cognitively impaired – all of which hype up our stress system.

The situation is worse for adolescents, because they require nine to ten hours sleep or they too will experience such difficulties. It is likely that most of our adolescents are up to ten hours sleep deprived each week.

The reasons for the sleep difficulties with this family are obvious. Firstly, all have their smart phones and other devices present in their rooms. Many of these emit blue wavelength light which reduces the ability of our brain to produce the neurotransmitter melatonin which is critical for sending us off to and keeping us asleep.

The second reason is that having the constant bleeping of smart phone SMS and email messages coming in and the temptation to check these devices early in the morning is often too much. This means we are not getting enough hours of sleep; and that we are also stressed and anxious about the content of emails and other messages received whilst not at work to sort problems out.

Thirdly, in relation to our children, by letting them have smart phones in their rooms at night, we are exposing them to constant interruptions to sleep and the potential for upsetting or bullying material to be beamed into their rooms, destroying their peace of mind and their sleep.

Obviously, we will start the day 'stressed out' if we have not have had enough sleep.

If we examine what happened at breakfast it is more of the same. Instead of the couple talking to both themselves and their adolescent children, they have allowed the 'machines' to encroach in on what should have been a bonding time and a chance for some quiet at the start of what will be a busy day. The children are learning at the feet of their masters. They are also falling into the peer group pressure trap of having to live every waking minute through social media. So, they too begin to assume that this is how life should be lived. By the end of breakfast all have become even more 'wired'. And the day has not even begun!

This meal scene is once again an example of what happens when couples and families are out in restaurants and cafes having meals together. I have often commentated on watching couples and indeed families and other groups out together with apparent objective of bonding but where all one sees are a group of heads down, smart phones out and the constant scrolling continuing!

Eating is one of the occasions when our stress system, through the parasympathetic nervous system (which we discussed earlier) gives our body and brain some 'down time'. It is not called the 'rest and digest' system for nothing. However, if even when eating we are still hyping up our stress system by constant monitoring of our phones, then toxic stress is not far away!

There is another issue with constant usage of technology in our homes: we are not exercising enough – the one thing that counteracts toxic stress the most! If we all were to examine how many hours of the day are filled with our interactions with machines and social media and how few with exercise, and do something about this imbalance, it might go a long way to reducing toxic stress.

It is also frightening to see how many of us on way to work, whether it is on the Tube, buses or trains or even when walking, are completely obsessed with our smart phones and social media. We are forgetting to look up, observe people, smell the roses and just enjoy the pleasure of being alive. Our stress system cannot take this continuous barrage and we are seeing the consequences all around us.

Some other issues of relevance from our tour are the areas of online social comparisons, cyberbullying, online pornography and pressures on young people in terms of sexuality.

We place enormous pressure on our shoulders on entering the world of comparing ourselves online either physically or in terms of how 'well' we seem to be doing in our lives. We are doomed to becoming stressed, anxious and on occasions even depressed if we play the 'rating game' which we will be discussing later in our step-by-step guide to dealing with toxic stress. This is a particular issue amongst our adolescent population but many adults are being sucked into this false world which promises much but just delivers unhappiness!

Technology also allows many forms of subtle bullying to go on. This cyberbullying can sometimes become extremely toxic, whether it be sharing inappropriate photos online, ganging up on colleagues or fellow students or revenge porn. The effects of this form of bullying on our stress system are extremely dangerous with our stress hormone levels constantly elevated. Many victims will fall foul of the worst symptoms of toxic stress and may find themselves constantly anxious, depressed and on some occasions suicidal.

Another major area of concern is the capacity for our smart phones and other devices to allow a constant flow of both porn and violent videos such as Isis beheadings to stream into our lives. It is rapidly becoming an area of stress for some of our young people, who are being forced by peer groups to take part in watching such material or be considered gay or mocked in some other manner. There are also the effects on our emotional brain if we give children as young as nine or ten such devices. This may be dooming them to toxic stress arriving in their lives at a very young age.

One must also worry about the potential loss of both empathy skills and indeed face-to-face interpersonal skills, both of which can end up creating significant stress in our lives. We cannot learn the skills of emotional learning through the medium of a machine!

Another area of potential stress is the area of online gambling addiction and the world of online gaming. The former can create enormous stress on both the addict and their families as it is so easy to run up huge debts. The latter can be equally damaging if we allow ourselves to be sucked into a world of spending up to ten hours a day living in this fantasy world. Our stress system is at a constant state of high alert as we play these games.

Finally, there is one other area involving technology that is leading to significant levels of toxic stress. This relates to the concept of 'disembodied services'. How often have we been left trying to contact a 'real human being' when attempting to sort out what should be a simple, routine issue. We find ourselves listening to 'please press one if you would like to – and two if you would like to – 'and so on till we get to the final piece' – all of our operators are busy now – please wait but please note that you can contact us online if you have any difficulties'. We then find ourselves listening to some classical music for up to half an hour. Many of us may find ourselves wanting to throw the phone at the wall in frustration at our inability to talk to a human being who can relate to us in a manner different from a machine. Those of us who have come up in gentler times also long for the soothing tones of somebody who might know what they are talking about – rather than a call centre situated in some far-off land!

This comes to a head when we enter the world for example of modern banking. Gone are the days when you could do your business in normal manner, lodging your money with a teller, discussing other issues with bank staff or on occasions the bank manager. Now it is like entering a new world where people to talk to are almost non-existent and at the centre lies the 'machine'. This machine is also finely tuned so the smallest error in trying to lodge money or cheques and all is spat back out. Older people are really stressed in coping with this new reality. The real agenda is of course to push us all online and to interact with the human face as little as is humanly possible. These changes are adding further stress to our already busy lives and for some can lead to further toxic stress.

And bit by bit as modern society travels rapidly down the road of increasingly disembodied services our stress system is also getting increasingly wired. Toxic stress is rarely far behind!

Before we leave this subject I want to acknowledge that there is of course much to be gained from our increasing use of technology and social media. I welcome for example the introduction of teaching children coding at school. But I do worry that increasingly we are using these mediums as an 'anaesthetic for life' and I feel that we must have a new conversation about their role. If not, then the toxic stress which is ensuing from their usage may be extremely damaging to our physical and mental health.

When automobiles were first introduced, we welcomed them with open arms. But as the roads became filled with cars and trucks, society quickly realized we had to create new 'rules of the road' to reduce injuries and fatalities. Perhaps the time has come to consider something similar for technology!

Later we will be showing how the step-by-step approach assisted some in learning how to reduce toxic stress in their lives by facing for the first time their over-reliance on these mediums.

# 6. THE DEADLY LINKS BETWEEN STRESS AND SUICIDE

Each year, more than fifty thousand people will self-harm in Ireland and between four hundred and six hundred will die by suicide. Stress is linked with these incidents to an increasing extent. The reason for this lies in the links between the individual's stress system and their brain. Depression can be triggered by chronic stress, and experiencing unhealthy stress as we are growing up results in changes in the brain which can predispose us to this illness. Post-mortem studies on victims of suicide have shown that the stress system has been activated for some time before death. These studies have found that the adrenal stress gland was increased in size, and that there were high levels of glucocortisol and stress peptides in the brain and body prior to suicide. This has been observed in a variety of mental-health problems, including depression, addiction, schizophrenia and personality disorder. In each case, stress seems to be triggering thoughts of self-harm and associated behaviours.

Responses to toxic stress often involve excessive alcohol consumption. This dramatically increases the risk of suicide, as alcohol prevents the logical brain from controlling impulsive thoughts and behaviour.

But why is toxic stress such a risk in relation to suicide? We know that all of us have a logical and an emotional brain. When we are emotionally well, the logical brain is able to keep the emotional brain 'in check'. Most mental illnesses relating to anxiety and depression occur due to a breakdown in this control mechanism. When we become significantly stressed, high glucocortisol levels, along with high stress peptide levels in the brain, tend to weaken and damage the crucial pathways between the emotional and the logical brain.

In depression in particular, the logical brain's control over self-harm thoughts and behaviour may be compromised. Those who would like to read more about these links should see my book *Flagging the Problem*.

We have gone through a seismic ten years in Ireland, the UK and many parts of the USA. A major financial and housing bubble in many developed countries burst leading to one of the most severe depressions in the past hundred years. During this ten years, housing shortages, mortgage difficulties, unemployment, financial difficulties, and relationship break-downs led to an epidemic of toxic stress. Young men under the age of thirty-five, many of whom felt disconnected from society, were particularly vulnerable to depression and often turned to alcohol. Thoughts of self-harm leading to suicide commonly followed. Even though many countries like Ireland have thankfully recovered from this terrible depression and employment is now almost back to where it was ten years ago, there is still a significant incidence of male suicide.

The reasons for this are quite complex. Unemployment is an obvious link between toxic stress and suicide. There is recent evidence from the Irish Suicidology Association of a two-to three-fold increase in suicide in men (and up to a six-fold increase in women) when unemployment is a factor. Clearly during the recession there was a concern with a rise in male suicide in both younger and older men in their fifties.

Even though financial and employment prospects have risen in some areas of the USA, UK and Ireland there are still many challenges left over from the terrible recession which even now has affected so many lives. Many families and individuals are still in debt. Young couples cannot buy houses and are being priced out of the rental sector leading to huge stress being placed on their young shoulders. Homelessness for families has increased. The impact of immigration is still being felt by many communities which were devastated and many towns and villages have been brought to their knees. Add into this mix the social changes brought in by technology and social media and the disappearance of meaning and sense of belonging for many young men and it is inevitable that toxic stress will rise and drag self-harm and suicide in its wake. Men will often not reveal their distress and end up getting into major difficulties – seeing suicide as the only way out.

Teaching people to recognize and deal with chronic stress could reduce the chances that they will end up in such situations and perhaps save lives. For as we will be discussing later, so much of the time it is our unhealthy interpretation of stressors in our lives that leads us into so much trouble. Learning to redefine stressors in a new way can completely transform how we deal with them.

We know from research that men and women are hard-wired differently, and that this is probably the main reason why men in these age groups exhibit a much higher risk of suicide. We know from national suicide statistics that four times as many young men die by suicide than women in the same age groups. In general, men are hard-wired to 'talk to themselves' rather than to others when they get into such stressful situations. The debate over whether such behavioural patterns are due to environmental influences during our upbringing or genetic/hormonal factors continues. In practice, although both are important, it seems likely that what happens hormonally in the womb is key.

GPs are also seeing older men and women struggling with similar stressors, particularly relating to personal debts, and being overwhelmed by them. The typical pattern is that toxic stress triggers depression, and in some cases suicide. As we have already mentioned, men often do not reveal their distress and end up getting into major difficulties, sometimes tragically seeing suicide as the only way out.

I think we also underestimate the importance of the emotion of 'shame' when discussing older age groups, particularly the forty-five-to-sixty-five bracket. Some, when faced with the shame of bankruptcy and possible loss of their income, their home and, most important of all, their self-esteem, may become overwhelmed, and see suicide as the only way out of the mire! There have been some very high-profile men who fit this pattern (e.g. Robert Maxwell).

Teaching people to identify and deal with chronic stress could reduce the chance that they will end up in these types of situations, and may potentially save lives. Redefining our interpretation of stressors can transform how we deal with stress. But to seriously challenge the carnage that chronic stress, leading to depression and suicide, is creating within our society is going to require a national change of policy. We need to learn from countries like Scotland (where they have absorbed all interested in suicide prevention under one organized, funded body) that have managed to create such a policy.

Above all, we need to create a safe environment for people experiencing toxic stress – whether it is through face-to-face consultations, telephone helplines, or monitored websites, internet chatrooms and bulletin boards.

## Toxic Stress – Can We Change?

Before moving on to examine a holistic approach to managing toxic stress we must answer the critical question as to whether it is possible for us to change our mind and brain to reduce or banish this menace from our lives.

The positive answer is that we can. Not only that, but we can bring in thinking and behavioural changes to reduce toxic stress in our lives and allow us to live happier more contented lives!

Many assume their upbringing is the cause of their toxic stress. Others assume that because they cannot change their past they are doomed to toxic stress for the future.

But this ignores one important crucial piece of information. Our brains are one of the most flexible and most adaptable organs ever created. We have the most extraordinary power to reshape our brains through the process called neuroplasticity. And what is even more extraordinary is that we can use the power of our own minds to reshape the pathways in our brain which are pushing us down the road of toxic stress.

Neuroplasticity describes the ability of individual neurons to increase/decrease the number of connections with other neurons and through this mechanism strengthen or weaken various brain pathways. Neuroplasticity therefore relates to the capacity of our brain to reshape its connections and pathways. Until recently it was assumed that when adult circuits in the brain were formed they were set for life. If our pathways predisposed us to anxiety, depression or toxic stress etc. we were doomed to follow where they led, for better or worse! We now know that this is not the case as the same mechanisms that helped form these paths can, through differing therapies, reshape them.

So even if we are predisposed to higher levels of toxic stress, we do have a secret weapon at our disposal, namely the power of our mind to use neuroplasticity to reshape our brain and our stress system. As we will now see, this is best done by using a holistic approach.

# 7. TOXIC STRESS:
# A HOLISTIC APPROACH

A therapeutic solution to toxic stress should follow a holistic approach. The various components of this approach in relation to stress are outlined below.

## Empathy

The ability to sense another person's emotional state can be a powerful healing tool. Most people innately possess this capacity. When choosing a health professional to help you deal with your distress, you must feel there is some sort of 'meeting of minds'. You should feel comfortable about opening up to this person before entering into a therapeutic relationship with them.

The key is to talk to somebody about how stressed you are feeling. It may be a partner or close friend or family member but you must feel comfortable that they will empathize with how you feel. Otherwise you will find yourself shutting down, as empathy is the doorway into our emotional mind. Some of us will be able to deal with chronic stress without feeling the need to work with a counsellor or therapist, but many will find the empathic bond which results from therapy helpful.

## Lifestyle

This plays a major role in the treatment and prevention of chronic stress. Research continues to emphasise the importance of exercise. What form of exercise is most beneficial, how often, and for how long, are questions exercising top research minds. The general consensus is as follows:

- Thirty minutes of brisk exercise, preferably three to five times a week, is ideal.
- Longer periods of exercise do not confer extra benefits.
- Any form of exercise – walking, jogging, weightlifting, swimming – is equally effective.
- Creative exercise, like dancing and water aerobics, is also effective and has the benefit of an extra social dimension.
- Staying close to nature (visiting forests, lakes and seascapes) is often overlooked in relation to preventing and treating toxic stress; combining this with exercise offers us the benefits of both!

But why is exercise so important in assisting us to deal with toxic stress in our lives? We now know that regular exercise increases levels of endorphin 'feel good' messengers in the brain, so we feel much more positive. It also reduces levels of our stress hormone glucocortisol and other stress peptides in the brain. It encourages the production of new nerve cells in an area of the brain called the hippocampus which is a major player in how we create, store and retrieve memories. We now know that toxic stress is particularly damaging to this part of the brain. Exercise also improves activity in our serotonin and dopamine systems in the brain which improve our mood and motivation. It also increases levels of BDNF (Brain-Derived Neurotrophic Factor) in the brain. This is one of the brain's most powerful weapons in staying healthy. It acts by improving the health of the neurons in the brain. The greater the expression of this protein in the brain, the healthier we become.

These effects of exercise are a powerful antidote to the multiple negative effects of toxic stress. The difficulties arise, as we will discuss later, when, because of this condition, we end up doing the opposite, becoming increasingly sedentary.

Diet is also important, as the brain is dependent on proper nutrition to function. A balanced diet when we are stressed can improve how we feel. I recommend the following:

- A sensible mix of fresh fish (particularly oily fish like salmon, mackerel and tuna), eggs (especially free-range), meat, vegetables, cereals, nuts, flax seeds and oils, grains and fruit
- Prepare your own food, and avoid fast food and highly processed foods as much as possible
- Eat, even when you are extremely stressed, as the brain cannot run without fuel
- Avoid high-stimulant drinks like coffee and Coke, which many with stress and anxiety use in abundance
- Avoid high-sugar 'hits', as fluctuating blood-sugar levels do not help good brain functioning
- Avoid the 'extreme diets' sometimes recommended by alternative 'experts', which often exclude key foods
- Avoid using food as a 'crutch' when feeling stressed or anxious
- The main supplements believed to promote mental health are Omega 3 fish oils, and the key B vitamins folic acid, B6 and B12. All of these have been extensively investigated and there is substantial evidence to support their use as part of a holistic approach to stress. I recommend a B-complex supplement daily and Omega 3 oils (particularly EPA), in a daily dose of 500-1000 mgs
- Pay special attention to the diet of young people (who are increasingly exposed to the ravages of toxic stress), which is often high in quantity and low in quality, at a critical stage of brain development

## Alternative Therapies

From the range of alternative therapies on offer, relaxation exercises, yoga, pilates and mindfulness are of proven benefit in treating toxic stress. Let's take a brief look at some of these therapies. What is very appealing to many people is the fact that these are natural therapies often make us 'feel better' about ourselves.

## Meditation

This is a mental technique which involves focusing the mind on an object, sound, prayer, breathing, or conscious thought, in order to increase our awareness of the present moment, help us to relax, reduce stress or enhance spiritual or personal growth. Of the alternative/complementary therapies on offer, this is the most interesting. It is a therapy with a sound scientific basis which has helped us understand the workings of the mind/brain in a different way. I have no hesitation in recommending it to all who suffer from stress.

In mental health, we have benefited from excellent research by Prof. Richard Davidson, who has examined what happens in the brain as a result of regular meditation. Because of his work, we now know that meditation shifts activity from the right side of the brain (the source of most of our negative thoughts and emotions) to the left. This explains the reduction in stress, increase in positive emotions like peacefulness, calmness, forgiveness, love, compassion and joy, reduction in negative thinking, and so on.

The practice of mindfulness is particularly worthwhile. Mindfulness is a form of meditation where we focus our mind on the present moment and are aware of our thoughts, emotions and body in the here and now, without passing judgement on ourselves. It has been shown to be a powerful tool in reducing the effects of toxic stress; it helps combat anxiety and depression, and even strengthens our immune system.

I often recommend the following simple 'Three-minute Breathing Space' exercise, and encourage you to build it into your everyday life. It can be done at any time of the day, and is particularly useful if you are under stress. It involves finding a quiet space for three minutes, adopting a comfortable posture and closing your eyes. Then you should do the following:

MINUTE 1: Focus your mind on inner experiences, your thoughts, emotions and physical sensations. Do not try to change or challenge them, just become aware of them.
MINUTE 2: Focus on the physical sensation of breathing, on the rise and fall of your chest with each breath. Again, do not try to control your breathing.
MINUTE 3: Become increasingly aware of your whole body, your posture, your facial expression and your bodily sensations. Accept how you are feeling without judgement.

## Yoga

This is an ancient Indian therapy which combines physical exercises, meditation and breathing techniques. The word itself means 'union', referring to the union of mind, body and spirit which has its base in ancient Hinduism. The combination of physical and breathing exercises can be used to reach meditative states. In the West, it is considered a form of physical exercise by many, but the relaxation/breathing exercises/meditation side of this therapy can be useful as a complementary therapy in stress. The main type of yoga used in the West is hatha yoga; it is based on bodily postures called 'Asanas', breathing exercises called 'Pranayama', and meditation.

## Aromatherapy

Aromatherapy is a therapy with roots in the ancient Persian, Greek and Roman eras. It is a 'scent-using therapy', with essential oils extracted from plants (leaves, flowers, roots, berries, and so on) being applied by massage, inhalation, or released into the atmosphere, with a view to treating various conditions. The theory behind this therapy is simple: the oils involved (absorbed through either the nose or the skin) arrive in the brain and have an effect on our stress system and mood. There is some evidence that aromatherapy acts as a 'relaxant', relieving symptoms of short-term stress.

## Massage

This is a popular therapy whose roots go back to ancient China, Egypt, Greece and Rome. There are a number of differing approaches, involving touching or kneading the skin, with a view to reducing pain, stress and anxiety.

## Aromatherapy Massage

This involves a combination of massage with aromatherapy oils, which we discussed earlier.

## Shiatsu

This is a Japanese massage therapy strongly influenced by Traditional Chinese Medicine, involving the use of hands (fingers/thumbs/palms), feet, knees, elbows, and so on, to massage various 'life energy' acupressure points. It is probably no more effective than simple massage.

## Indian Head Massage

This is another popular therapy, with its origins in Ayurvedic Traditional Medicine. It involves massaging the scalp, neck, face, ears and shoulders, to induce a profound state of relaxation.

## Reflexology

Reflexology involves applying finger/thumb pressure to the soles of the feet, which are thought to be connected to different parts of the body through the nervous system. The concept that particular pressure points on the foot correspond to various parts of the body and can be used to diagnose illnesses has been scientifically disproved. In practice, it is much more likely that the biological effects of massage in general are the reason for any success achieved by reflexology in reducing stress.

The role of spirituality and religion in acting as a bulwark against toxic stress is often overlooked. Many people find that time spent in contemplation is both rejuvenating and stress-reducing.

## Sleep

We need to pay particular attention to the importance of sleep in the treatment of toxic stress. Sleep is vital for our physical and mental health: we all need approximately eight hours of sleep a night. When we are stressed, we struggle to sleep – even though we may feel exhausted. To improve our chance of a good night's sleep, the following advice may be helpful:

- Try to go to bed at a consistent hour – preferably before midnight.
- Try and exercise for thirty minutes a day.
- Avoid stimulants like tea and coffee.
- Be wary of using alcohol as an aid to sleep – this may lead to misuse and abuse.

- Avoid reading for any period in bed – unless the book is boring.
- Avoid watching TV or a DVD just before going to bed.
- Do yoga/mindfulness exercises before going to bed.
- If taking a midday nap, keep it to ten minutes or less.
- Try to sleep in an airy, well-ventilated room.
- Think about taking melatonin supplements.
- If problems persist, see your family doctor.
- Remember that major sleep difficulties can be a warning sign of depression as well as chronic stress.
- Create a technology free bedroom.

Any holistic package designed to deal with stress must involve reviewing stress factors in our lives and being honest with ourselves and those around us. We must not be afraid to make major changes in employment, relationships, and financial matters. These issues will be examined in more detail later.

## Drug Therapy

This is of limited benefit in chronic stress, unless the person has also developed depression, in which case it can be extremely effective. Tranquillizers are not recommended, as they carry a risk of addiction.

## Talk Therapy

This is, along with lifestyle changes, the therapy of choice for the management of toxic stress. For those who are experiencing stress, talk therapy can be an extremely good way of dealing with underlying problems.

Talk therapy, often called 'psychotherapy', is a means of treating psychological or emotional problems through verbal and non-verbal communication. It involves talking with a specially trained therapist and learning new ways of coping with distress. The immediate goal is to help the person increase their self-knowledge and their awareness of their relationships with others.

Psychotherapy helps people become more aware of their unconscious thoughts, feelings and motives. Its long-term goal is to make it possible to exchange destructive patterns of behaviour for healthier, more successful ones. There are many different forms of talk therapy, including counselling, psychoanalytic psychotherapy, cognitive behaviour therapy, behaviour therapy, interpersonal therapy, supportive psychotherapy, brief dynamic psychotherapy, and family therapy.

All of these have a place in the management of toxic stress, but two stand out: cognitive behaviour therapy and counselling in all its forms. We will be demonstrating the value of the former in the second part of this book.

Now that we have a deeper understanding of toxic stress and its effects, let's move on to a new seven-step approach to dealing with this potentially lethal condition.

# PART TWO

This section will introduce a simple seven-step programme which aims to help us recognise and deal with toxic stress. This approach, which is based on the concept of self-sufficiency, involves understanding how stress affects us personally, and developing techniques to deal with it. I will outline many common examples of everyday stress in the hope that the reader may identify with them and find them useful.

## Dr Bill, the Stress-Buster

In the following examples, our health professional demonstrating how to deal with a range of stressful situations will be 'Dr Bill'. Dr Bill specialises in stress management and its effects on mental and physical health. He suggests cognitive and behavioural changes, which aim to help his patients deal more effectively with stress. He will be using simple CBT concepts – in particular the 'ABC' approach discussed above. His overall approach is based on a realistic appraisal of the person's situation, and he employs holistic solutions to 'detoxify' stress.

To benefit significantly from the seven-step program, you must be honest with yourself and accept that serious changes in many aspects of your life may be required. Changing the brain for the better requires significant changes to a person's behaviour. If you are not prepared to tackle key issues, you will struggle to deal with toxic stress. On the other hand, if you are prepared to put the effort in, you will experience profound benefits to your physical and psychological well-being.

# STEP ONE
# IDENTIFYING TOXIC STRESS

For some, the first wake-up call that stress is a problem will involve ending up in a hospital following a heart attack! For others, it may involve succumbing to a significant viral infection or debilitating mental illness such as depression. We often ignore obvious warning signs, as heeding them will require serious changes in our lives. The first step in our programme is learning to recognise these warning signs. These signs can be divided into the following categories:

- Physical symptoms
- Psychological symptoms
- Unhealthy behaviours

## Physical Symptoms

- Difficulty sleeping, waking up throughout the night, grinding teeth when asleep, and having nightmares
- Persistent tension headaches
- Abdominal symptoms such as constipation, diarrhoea, stomach pains and cramps
- Symptoms of anxiety such as sweating, palpitations, shortness of breath and deep sighing
- Muscle tension and muscle pain
- Bouts of viral and bacterial illnesses
- Loss of libido

- Obesity or weight loss
- Restlessness

## Psychological Symptoms

- Chronic fatigue or exhaustion, often mistaken for physical fatigue
- Frustration, anger and intolerance
- Anxiety
- Feelings of hopelessness, worthlessness and helplessness
- Depression, and negative and suicidal thoughts
- Fixed ways of thinking, which can create problems at home and at work
- Poor decision-making
- Addiction
- Impaired short-term memory

## Unhealthy Behaviours

- Smoking and excessive alcohol consumption
- Inactivity
- Not eating properly
- Use of stimulants such as caffeine or energy drinks to combat fatigue
- Using drugs such as hash or cocaine, or becoming addicted to prescription medication
- Staying up late at night
- Spending too much time on inappropriate internet sites – many of which may not be helpful
- Constant negative rumination on the problems facing us

If any of these symptoms or behaviours applies to you, take out a pen and paper and write them down. Identifying these symptoms is the first step towards recovery. The next step involves ruling out physical and psychological illnesses which may account for the distress. A visit to the family doctor may be necessary to complete this step. Your doctor may order a blood test, which can be helpful in two ways. First, you may suffer from a common condition which explains your symptoms. Secondly, if you are suffering from toxic stress, it may detect physical consequences arising from it.

The following conditions are easily diagnosed with a blood test, and should be ruled out before diagnosing stress:

- ANAEMIA, resulting from iron deficiency. This is more common in women (usually due to heavy periods) than men.
- DIABETES, which may present with fatigue, thirst, and abdominal pains.
- THYROID DISEASE, where an underactive thyroid may result in weight loss, tremors, fatigue and feeling too hot. An overactive thyroid may result in weight gain, feeling cold, sluggishness, fatigue, coarse dry skin and hair loss.

Two psychological conditions often confused with chronic stress are generalised anxiety disorder and depression (major depressive disorder).

GENERALISED ANXIETY DISORDER (GAD) can present with some or all of these symptoms:

- intense anxiety and foreboding
- excessive worry about health, family or job issues
- a constant sense of impending disaster
- mental or physical fatigue
- impaired memory and concentration
- muscle tension, restlessness and tremors
- sleep difficulties, nightmares and teeth grinding
- indecisiveness, avoiding new situations or starting new tasks
- irritable bowel symptoms, tension headaches, sighing and palpitations
- loss of appetite and weight loss or weight gain

MAJOR DEPRESSIVE DISORDER (MDD) can present with some or all of the following symptoms:

- extreme low mood for a period of more than two weeks
- extreme fatigue – usually much more severe than in GAD
- anxiety
- weight loss or weight gain
- poor concentration and poor short-term memory
- loss of self-esteem
- reduced drive and libido
- loss of pleasure
- sleep difficulties – particularly early-morning wakening
- negative thoughts about ourselves, those close to us and the world in general – the typical ones being 'I'm worthless' and 'The world would be better off without me'
- suicidal thoughts, plans or actions

It is obvious that chronic stress, generalised anxiety disorder and depression share certain symptoms. So how can you tell them apart?

Depression is the simplest disorder to identify. Symptoms such as severe and persistent drops in mood, energy levels, concentration, drive, sleep and appetite are much more pronounced than in the other conditions. Most people suffering from chronic stress are able to get on with their lives, but those with depression may struggle to cope. Chronic stress is now recognised as a precursor to depression. What differentiates the two conditions are the severity of symptoms in those who are depressed, and a lack of any obvious trigger in depression.

It is more difficult to separate GAD from chronic stress, as the symptoms are remarkably similar. Many therapists feel that stress and anxiety are two sides of the same coin. However, chronic stress usually has a clear, identifiable cause, whereas those suffering from GAD will have a history of worrying, foreboding and fearfulness, without any obvious trigger. One can usually associate chronic stress with particular events and stressors.

As all three conditions result in increased levels of glucocortisol, their negative consequences on physical and psychological well-being are similar. The treatments for the three conditions differ, though, so accurate diagnosis is of paramount importance. Let's look at a few examples.

## 'I Just Feel So Tired'

Mary is thirty-one and struggles with looking after three small children and working part-time in a busy office. She comes to see Dr Bill complaining of constant fatigue over the previous three months. 'There has to be something physically wrong with me,' she says. 'It's not normal to feel like this.'

On further questioning, she reveals a host of other symptoms. She is sleeping poorly, suffering from nightmares and waking with jaw pain each morning. She feels irritable and on edge, and has lost weight. She also notes that her concentration at work has waned: she has been pulled up on a number of occasions over errors she has made. This has only worsened her feelings. Her best friend was worried that she had become depressed and had persuaded her to visit Dr Bill. Mary was concerned herself because her mother had died in her fifties from a stroke. Her life is stressful: she is on the go from early morning and collapses into bed, exhausted, every night. She admits to drinking and smoking more than she used to. Her husband is doing his best to help, but she feels overwhelmed.

Dr Bill rules out depression and, although she has some symptoms of anxiety, decides that she does not meet the criteria for GAD. Further examination rules out obvious physical symptoms such as high blood pressure. A blood test indicates that she does not suffer from anaemia, diabetes or thyroid disease. He explains to Mary that she is exhibiting all the signs of chronic stress. Mary has now achieved the first objective, in that she has finally identified the cause of her fatigue.

## 'I Have Lost Interest in Everything'

Jim's wife encourages him to make an appointment with Dr Bill, as she has become increasingly concerned about his lack of interest in activities. There is a family history of diabetes, and although Jim is only forty, she has become convinced that this must be the underlying problem.

Like most men, Jim finds it difficult to talk about how he feels. However, he gradually begins to open up to Dr Bill about his various symptoms. He says he is constantly fatigued and on edge, is eating and drinking too much, and is tired no matter how much he sleeps. His libido has plummeted over the previous six months: he says he has 'no interest' in sex. He admits that he is often worried and finds it difficult to concentrate. He says he doesn't feel depressed but just 'not himself'. He finally blurts out that he has struggled with dealing with being put on part-time hours at work, saying: 'I just can't cope.'

After further examination and some blood tests, Dr Bill explains that Jim's loss of drive is not due to any physical illness. He warns him, however, that his eating patterns are predisposing him to this in the future due to his family history. Dr Bill excludes depression and explains that Jim is suffering from chronic stress brought on by fears that he will lose his job. Jim has begun the first part of the journey back to health: identifying the cause of his stress.

## 'I Must Have A Brain Tumour'

Sue presents to Dr Bill complaining of persistent headaches over the previous month. She is a twenty-seven-year-old secretary who works for a company that is struggling to survive the negative effects of the recent recession. She is convinced that the headaches have a sinister cause and breaks down in tears. She admits to being constantly fatigued, picking at her food, being irritable with her partner, and having a constant feeling of butterflies in her stomach. She tosses and turns at night and is taking large quantities of painkillers. She does not feel depressed but is not enjoying life as much as she used to. The headaches are starting to take over her life, and her concentration and memory are suffering. Her mother had suffered from chronic anxiety but Sue doesn't feel that she is an 'anxious person'. She admits that her workplace is a source of increasing stress for her and is concerned about the risks of the business folding.

Dr Bill checks that her blood pressure is normal. He rules out migraine and decides to refer her for a brain scan to eliminate any serious conditions, such as a tumour. All comes back clear. He then explains that her headaches are due to chronic stress and that eliminating this stress will involve tackling the underlying causes. Sue realises that her headaches do not have a sinister cause, but are the result of stress.

## 'I Am Constantly Sick'

Matt arrives to see Dr Bill with a long list of low-grade infections. He has been experiencing cold sores, mouth ulcers, chest infections and stomach upsets. He is worried that there must be some serious underlying problem. On further questioning, he admits to constant fatigue, and that he has been drinking alcohol in large quantities. He has also been sleeping poorly and has had a lot of muscle pain and numerous low-grade headaches.

Matt is a mechanic; he is working longer hours due to the difficulties the motor industry is facing. He commutes long distances to work and is generally irritable and tired upon returning home. Following a thorough examination, Dr Bill sends Matt for blood tests. When the results return clear, Dr Bill explains that chronic stress is a common cause of the symptoms of which he is complaining. Matt was concerned about his family history of heart disease. Dr Bill explains that stress itself could increase his risk of heart disease and that he would have to make major changes to his life in order to deal with the problem. Matt has learnt how important it is to identify chronic stress in his life – which is the first step towards a return to health.

### 'My Employer Has Sent me Here!'

Tom's boss refers him to see Dr Bill. He is extremely put out by the fact that he has to attend as he is a 'very busy man'. His boss has sent him to the doctor because Tom had mentioned in passing that he was experiencing chest pains. Tom is an extremely successful businessman, but is renowned for having a very short fuse. In Tom's world, everything had to be done 'yesterday'. He felt that he was just wasting the doctor's time – and, more importantly, his own.

Dr Bill notes that Tom's father had suffered a major heart attack in his fifties but had survived it – only to die five years later from a massive stroke. On further questioning, Tom admits that he is smoking forty cigarettes a day and drinking significantly more alcohol than the recommended weekly limit. When the word 'stress' is mentioned, Tom starts laughing: 'I wouldn't know what the word means. That's for weaklings.' It becomes obvious he has a type A personality, and that his father probably had a similar disposition. Dr Bill is concerned about Tom's chest pains and notes that Tom's blood pressure is elevated and that his blood fats are very high. He decides to send Tom to a cardiologist, who puts three stents into his coronary arteries. Tom arrives back to Dr Bill a chastened man: the cardiologist has explained how close he was to a major, life-threatening event. Dr Bill goes on to explain the concept of toxic stress and the dangers of having a type A personality; he tells Tom that his lifestyle is putting his health at risk. At the root of Tom's problem lies his demand that the world must change to suit him – an approach which can be described as 'low frustration tolerance'. Tom also grasps that his unhealthy lifestyle is having an adverse impact on his health. Tom argues that he is too busy to change, but Dr Bill points out that the cemetery is full of very busy young men. This is the start of Tom's journey towards a new life.

### 'I Just Feel Terrible!'

Monica comes to see Dr Bill but struggles to explain what is wrong with her. 'I just feel terrible!' she exclaims. She is a thirty-two-year-old mother of one. Both her partner and herself are working a three-day week. Money is tight – they are barely able to make the mortgage repayments – and they are both afraid of losing their jobs. She assumes that she is suffering from stress: she complains of feeling very down and exhausted, is struggling to eat, sleep or concentrate, and has lost all interest in life. Were it not for her three-year-old child, she would consider 'ending it all'. After saying this, she breaks down. She feels ashamed that she could even think like this, as she has a loving husband, a beautiful child, and is lucky to have a job. With Dr Bill's help, she soon realises that she is not suffering from stress, but from depression. It emerges that there is a history of depression: her mother had been hospitalised for severe postnatal depression. Monica had initially been experiencing stress, but after a prolonged period had slowly slipped into depression. Her journey involves first dealing with her depression, and then later developing more effective ways of coping with stress.

### 'I am Spending My Day on the Loo!'

Bob arrives to see Dr Bill in an exasperated state after a two-year battle with abdominal pains, cramps and alternating constipation and diarrhoea. 'It is taking over my life,' he explains. He is working in a busy insurance company and is under a lot of pressure there. He explains that 'results are everything' and reveals that, so far, five of his colleagues have been let go. He feels ashamed of his problem and is increasingly concerned about the possibility of cancer, as his father died of bowel cancer. Due to this family history, Dr Bill sends Bob for a colonoscopy; the results come back clear. Dr Bill explains the concept of chronic stress and how it is often related to anxiety. He explains that Bob's emotional brain was triggering his symptoms, as it controls the nerve supply to his bowel, resulting in persistent stimulation of the bowel. Bob's journey will involve an understanding of the way in which his desire for complete certainty in his life resulted in his bowel becoming overactive. He grasps that he needs to learn to understand how stress is impinging on his life and how to develop coping mechanisms to deal with it.

### 'I Get so Stressed'

James, a forty-four-year-old plumber, presents to Dr Bill complaining of feeling 'stressed all the time'. On further questioning, it turns out that he is a passive partner in a very manipulative marriage where his wife is very domineering. Throughout his life, he has failed to stand up for himself – both at work and at home. James's father had been of a similar disposition and had died in his fifties. Although James was concerned about this, he was more stressed about his unhealthy relationship. After discussing matters with Dr Bill, he discovered that his upbringing and personality had led him to be less assertive, resulting in toxic stress. Dr Bill explains that through assertiveness training and a lot of hard work, James would not only feel better about himself but would also improve his physical well-being. After using assertiveness techniques learned on a course, he faced up to people who had made his life a misery including his wife – and they tended to back down.

### 'I Find Social Situations Stressful But Just Bottle it Up'

Louise, a thirty-three-year-old executive, comes to see Dr Bill complaining of feeling stressed, particularly in social situations. She dreads attending social events, and relives her performance afterwards. 'I am like a cut-down version of my father,' she notes gloomily, 'and look how long he lasted.' It turns out that her father had also dreaded social situations, and had turned to alcohol to cope with them. He died of a massive heart attack at age sixty. Louise is smoking heavily and, like her father, drinks too much at social situations to cover up her feelings of social inadequacy. Of particular concern is her negative assessment of herself and her future as a result of the social difficulties she is experiencing. Dr Bill also wonders about type D personality traits, and the potential dangers associated with them. He shows her how simple CBT exercises can help her deal with her social anxiety and transform her life. He also advises her to change her lifestyle, in particular her smoking.

It is clear from the above examples that stress can present itself in varied forms and can threaten a person's physical health as well as their psychological well-being. If you can relate to any of the above stories, you have taken the important first step of recognising that stress is a problem for you. The second step – learning to identify the thoughts, emotions and behaviours underlying the chronic stress you are experiencing – is as simple as 'ABC', as we will see!

# STEP TWO
# DEALING WITH OUR THOUGHTS, EMOTIONS AND BEHAVIOUR – THE 'ABC' MODEL

The psychotherapist Albert Ellis transformed the way we deal with thoughts, emotions and behaviour by devising the 'ABC' model. This model is particularly useful when coping with stress. Let's start by defining our thoughts, emotions and behaviours.

THOUGHTS are best defined as 'the words, images, ideas, memories, beliefs and concepts that flow in and out of our conscious mind'. It is important to note the following:

- Just because a thought comes into our mind does not mean it is true.
- Thoughts rarely exist alone but usually arrive in a flow, one quickly following another, in what's known as a 'cascade effect'.
- Sometimes we can get seemingly random 'automatic thoughts' passing through our mind at lightning speed. It is very important to become aware of these thoughts.
- Thoughts can be visual, logical or emotional in nature.
- Thoughts influence emotions, which in turn influence behaviours.
- While there is a major emphasis on positive vs. negative thoughts when dealing with mental health, perhaps the concept of 'realistic thoughts' is more useful when dealing with stress.

EMOTIONS relate to how we feel, and last for relatively short durations, usually minutes or hours. If a particular emotion lasts for longer periods, i.e. hours to days, we call them moods. Some experts combine emotions and moods, calling them 'feelings'. I have always preferred to keep these separate, as it reduces confusion. The rich tapestry of life is created through our emotions, as a world without them would be grey and empty. Emotions can be categorised as follows:

- POSITIVE EMOTIONS include joy, happiness, pleasure, love, awe, trust, contentment and peacefulness.
- NEGATIVE EMOTIONS include anger, fear, guilt, shame, hurt, jealousy, emotional pain, sadness and loss.
- HEALTHY EMOTIONS include grief and loss, sadness, disappointment, annoyance, frustration and irritation, regret and remorse.
- UNHEALTHY EMOTIONS include anxiety, depression, anger, emotional pain, shame, guilt, jealousy, envy and hurt.

The following are some important characteristics of emotions:

- Emotions are associated with physical symptoms. Fear is associated with palpitations, dry mouth and shallow breathing. Depression is associated with tiredness and sleep and appetite problems.
- Emotions can be negative but not unhealthy. Anger, guilt, sadness and loss are normal, healthy emotions following the death of a loved one.
- Just because emotions are negative or unhealthy does not mean that the person experiencing them is distressed or unwell.
- Emotions heavily influence our behaviour. If we are sad, we may cry; if we are angry, we may become aggressive.
- The decisions we make in life are more influenced by emotions than logic.
- Modern therapists believe that suppressing emotions is unwise and recommend that we accept and embrace them.
- While a great deal of emphasis is placed on the role of negative emotions in illnesses like depression and anxiety, it is often forgotten how powerful

positive emotions such as love, hope, joy, compassion, trust and forgiveness can be in our lives. We know about the power of positive thinking, but need to hear more about the power of positive emotions! This is especially relevant when dealing with stress.

- Many emotions ascribed to thoughts and events are sourced in unconscious emotional memory created during upbringing and adult life. These emotions may be triggered by internal or external events.

- Emotions and thoughts are interconnected. Many people assume that our emotions control our thoughts. At first glance, this seems to be true, but many emotional responses to situations are based on thoughts or beliefs. It is the *interaction* between thoughts and emotions which will determine our mental health and how we cope with stressors.

BEHAVIOUR is best defined as 'what we do in response to events occurring in our internal or external environment'. It can be influenced by both logic and emotion. The following are some important characteristics of behaviour:

- Behaviour can be healthy or unhealthy. Typical examples of unhealthy behaviour in depression are misuse of alcohol and self-harm. Typical examples of unhealthy behaviour in anxiety are misuse of tranquillizers, and avoidant or perfectionist behaviour. Violence is an example of unhealthy behaviour in response to anger.

- We can change behaviour even if we are struggling to change thoughts and emotions. Changing behaviour can be a powerful tool in treating anxiety and depression. A good example of this is encouraging those with depression to exercise – which in turn helps lift mood. We can't *think* our way into right being – but we can *act* our way into right thinking. This can also be applied to toxic stress.

- We can indirectly change behaviour by changing thoughts and emotions.

- Safety behaviour is a common coping strategy used by a person to prevent them experiencing a distressing emotion, such as those experiencing panic attacks using tranquillizers.

- Avoidant behaviour is another coping strategy; this includes avoiding public areas in phobia or avoiding exercise in depression. These behaviours are also observed in chronic stress.

Ellis's insight was that it is not what happens to us in life that upsets us and causes us grief, but rather how we *interpret* what happens. This interpretation arises from belief systems we develop over the course of our lives. These beliefs can often be compared to a virus we pick up without noticing it, and which then begins to spread through all areas of our lives.

Ellis also demonstrated that the resulting emotions we feel, and the physical symptoms which accompany them, have particular behavioural consequences. It is often the physical symptoms or negative behaviours arising from our emotions that encourage us to come for help. He developed a simple 'ABC' approach.

## A stands for ACTIVATING EVENT

This starts a particular chain of thoughts, emotions and behaviour. It can refer to an external event, either existing or anticipated, or an internal one, such as a memory, mental image, particular thought or dream. A useful way of examining the activating event is to divide it into:

- THE TRIGGER, which relates to the actual event which begins the process
- THE INFERENCE we draw from this trigger; in other words, how we interpret the event which has occurred. In many cases, this involves assigning a 'danger' to the triggering event. We need to understand why this event is bothering us.

## B stands for BELIEF

Belief encompasses our thoughts, the demands we place on ourselves and our world, our attitudes, and the meaning we attach to internal and external events in our lives. We interpret the trigger described above through these beliefs. Ellis divided these beliefs into two groups: rational and irrational.

These were described as follows by a fellow colleague of mine, Dr Paul

Gannon, an Irish GP who specialises in occupational medicine:

- RATIONAL BELIEFS (in relation to ourselves, others or the world in general) are those which lead to healthy negative emotions like anger, concern and sadness. These beliefs are self-limiting, problem-solving and empowering. They are a result of the person adopting a non-demanding philosophy and help us adapt to life events.
- IRRATIONAL BELIEFS (in relation to ourselves, others or the world in general) are those that lead to unhealthy negative emotions like rage, anxiety and depression. They are self-defeating, problem-generating and disabling, and impair our ability to cope.

## C stands for CONSEQUENCES

This which represents the emotional and behavioural responses which arise from 'A' and 'B' above. An example of this would be Joe, who is due to sit his driving test in two days' time. He becomes very stressed and anxious. If we were carrying out an 'ABC' analysis of his problem, it would look like this:

A   Activating Event:
- Trigger: his upcoming test
- Inference/danger: He might not pass his test.

B   Belief/Demands: He must pass his test; if he doesn't, he will be a failure.

C   Consequences:
- Emotion: anxiety
- Physical reactions: His stomach is in knots; he has a tension headache and is sighing constantly.
- Behaviour: stops eating, as his stomach is upset, and wonders if he should find an excuse to cancel the test

Another simple example of this would be when Sara finds out that a work colleague is about to lose her job. In this case, her 'ABC' would look like this:

A   Activating Event:
  - Trigger: her work colleague being let go
  - Inference/Danger: the thought that she might be next to lose her job

B   Belief/Demands: She must be completely certain that she will not be fired; if she is fired, she won't be able to cope with being unemployed.

C   Consequences:
  - Emotion: anxiety
  - Physical reactions: Her stomach is in knots; she has a tension headache and is sighing constantly.
  - Behaviour: stops eating, as her stomach is upset; tries excessively hard to please her boss; constantly rings a friend who works in personnel, seeking reassurance; begins to look up future job options, and is constantly checking her finances

In further steps, we will show you how to apply this ABC model to yourself. But first let's look at other common examples of chronic stress which present to Dr Bill, and how he uses the 'ABC' approach to tease out the problems.

### 'I Feel Trapped'

George is sent by the company doctor to see Dr Bill, as he was complaining of fatigue. He was falling behind in his work projects and had become increasingly irritable and snappy with work colleagues. He had been fully investigated physically, so Dr Bill decides to do an 'ABC' on the problem. They agree on the following:

A   Activating Event:
- Trigger: an increasing workload created by the retirement of two senior colleagues, with an embargo on new employees
- Inference/Danger: All responsibility was being passed on to him, doubling of his workload; he was 'trapped' in this situation, as jobs were very scarce; if he complained and was let go, he would not be able to look after his family.

B    Belief/Demands: He must not lose his job.

C    Consequences:
- Emotion: anxiety, chronic stress and low mood, and anger towards his employers
- Physical reactions: fatigue, headaches and muscle tension
- Behaviour: muses constantly about losing his job; tries excessively hard to complete his work projects perfectly; becomes irritable with colleagues due to exhaustion and frustration; sleeps poorly; stops eating healthy food; smokes more; ceases to exercise, and starts looking for a new job

## 'We Will End Up on the Streets!'

Mary attends Dr Bill with a host of physical symptoms. After taking her history, conducting a physical exam and doing some tests, he quickly realises that she is suffering from chronic stress and anxiety. The stressor was a common one, namely housing. They decide to work together on an 'ABC' of the problem, which went as follows:

A    Activating Event:
- Trigger: she and her partner have fallen behind on their mortgage repayments and are receiving letters from the bank regarding their situation.
- Inference/Danger: They may not be able to reach a compromise with the bank; as a result, they may end up in court and find themselves homeless.

B    Belief/Demands: They must be able to meet their repayments.

C    Consequences:
- Emotions: anxiety, chronic stress and low mood
- Physical reactions: fatigue, headaches, muscle tension, weight loss due to lack of interest in food, and facial pain resulting from grinding teeth at night
- Behaviour: ruminates constantly on the fear of losing her house; ignores

any new post in case it brings bad news; stops eating and can't sleep at night, and rings her sister constantly looking for reassurance

## 'I Just Can't Concentrate!'

Peter, a student, is reaching the end of an intensive three-year PhD, but attends Dr Bill complaining of a lack of energy and concentration. This is a problem, as he has only three months to finish his thesis before his funding runs out. He has become convinced that some serious physical illness is underlying his symptoms and has come for a check-up. Following some tests, Dr Bill says that Peter's problems are caused by chronic stress. They apply the following 'ABC' to his situation:

A   Activating Event:
- Trigger: finishing his PhD
- Inference/Danger: He may not be able to complete his PhD properly and in time, and as a result may not succeed in obtaining the qualification; his funding may run out before he can finish his thesis.

B   Belief/Demands: He must complete his PhD within the timeframe allowed.

C   Consequences:
- Emotions: anxiety, chronic stress
- Physical reactions: fatigue, headaches, muscle tension, weight loss due to lack of interest in food, constantly feeling 'wired'
- Behaviour: ruminates constantly about what will happen if he is not awarded his PhD; frets about what he will do if his funding runs out; eats too much junk food; procrastinates; stops exercising; drinks more alcohol, and smokes marijuana in an attempt to relax

## 'I Just Can't Go On!'

Joan comes to see Dr Bill at the end of a five-year period in which she has struggled to deal with her alcoholic husband, whose drinking has left the family facing financial ruin. She has only remained in the marriage for the sake of her two teenage girls, but the stress of the situation has worn her down, and a combination of physical and psychological symptoms have forced her to come for help. It becomes obvious that she has been suffering from chronic stress. To help her deal with the issue, Dr Bill does an 'ABC' of her problem:

A   Activating Event:
- Trigger: living with an alcoholic husband
- Inference/Danger: Her husband is never going to change; she will be trapped in the situation because of her two children; at some point, she will cease to be able to cope with the situation.

B   Belief/Demands: Her husband must change his behaviour; if he does not, she might have to consider leaving him.

C   Consequences:
- Emotions: anxiety, chronic stress, anger and low mood
- Physical reactions: fatigue, headaches, muscle tension, weight loss due to lack of interest in food
- Behaviour: thinks constantly about feeling trapped; eats and sleeps poorly; smokes; stops exercising, and constantly fights with her husband over his drinking

It is obvious from all of the above examples that the source of chronic stress lies in our interpretation of a stressor, and, as a result, the demands we place on ourselves and the situations in which we find ourselves. We can also see that it is usually the physical symptoms which arise from this stress that lead us to seek help, and that our behaviour often only makes matters worse. Managing toxic stress is not just about identifying our patterns of thought and behaviour; we must also learn to challenge these patterns. So let's move on to examining how we might do this.

# STEP THREE
# CHALLENGING OUR INTERPRETATION
# OF STRESSORS

We are all presented with a complex series of stressors throughout our lives. Often these stressors can be serious in nature, but our interpretations of what should be relatively innocuous stressors can lead us into just as much difficulty as the stressors themselves. The secret to understanding and dealing with toxic stress in our lives is to learn to logically evaluate stress triggers. One of the best ways of doing this is to visualise what will happen as a result of being exposed to this stressor. People have active imaginations, and a great capacity for concocting elaborate stories and mental images. However, just because we predict that a scenario will turn out a certain way does not mean that this will be the case.

Realising that these visualisations can give us a false impression of where we are now, or what will happen in the future, opens up a new way of thinking about – and dealing with – stressors. The problem is that we often develop set ways of thinking about things, which are difficult to challenge.

The good news is that, with commitment and hard work, it is possible to 'mute' the negative stress responses to events in our lives. It is also important to note that everyone is different, and what is stressful for one person is not for another. People often find it difficult to grasp that other people do not get stressed in situations that might cause us great stress. The complex interaction between genes and the environment is different for each individual. Consider the following examples, involving five people who lose their job at the same company, but have different interpretations of this stressor.

### 'This is a Disaster!'

Mary is devastated. Fortunately, she is only renting an apartment, but in her mind she already considers herself homeless. She anticipates that she will be unable to find another job, and so will not be able to pay her rent and will have to move out of her flat and return home to live with her parents. She predicts that she will be trapped in this situation for the foreseeable future. Her parents' home is fifty miles away from where she currently lives, and that will mean that her new boyfriend will definitely leave her. For her, losing her job is a disaster with which she will be unable to cope. While losing a job is stressful, Mary's *interpretation* of what will happen as a result is triggering chronic stress, despite the fact that she has no proof that these things will happen.

### 'How Dare They Fire Me!'

John is furious. He is an ambitious businessman and believed that he was invaluable to the company. He considers himself much more able than some employees who were not let go. He reckons he will easily find another job; what bothers him is the insult of being fired. For John, the fear of unemployment is not a major stressor. However, the feeling that he has been mistreated could trigger a bout of stress over the coming months.

### 'This May Present Me With an Opportunity!'

Peter, who works at management level, hears the news and is initially quite concerned about the potential consequences. He is married with two small children and has a mortgage to pay. But after the initial shock subsides, he begins to see an opportunity in the redundancy offer. He had been unhappy in his current situation for quite some time and had already begun to seek out contacts in the business world with a view to moving 'sideways'. Peter realises that he can pay off some of his mortgage with the redundancy money and begins to seek alternative employment. He has been able to interpret his job loss in a positive way, thereby neutralising the stressor.

### 'I am too Old to Find Another Job!'

Maura is devastated by the news. She is fifty, and her job is very important to her. It has helped her pay her bills, and provided her with a social network and a reason to get up every morning. But what is really bothering her about losing her job is her age: in her mind, she has no hope of finding work again, particularly in the current economic environment. She starts to visualise herself at home, alone, bored and unable to look after herself financially. In fact, Maura has no proof that her visualisation will come true, or that she will never be employed again. But she is so convinced that this will be the case that she slips into a bout of chronic stress and develops an alcohol addiction.

### 'We Will Lose the House!'

James feels as if his world has collapsed around him. He is happily married, with two kids just about to go to college, and still has a significant amount to pay on his mortgage. He is forty-seven and, like Maura, feels that his chances of getting another job are slim. But while he is concerned about his children and paying for their college education, his primary fear is that he and his wife will be unable to pay the mortgage on the house and that they will be forced to hand it back to the bank. He begins to create in his mind a nightmare scenario: the letters from the bank, the debt collectors at the house, the legal proceedings, and the pitying looks from family and friends. These thoughts overwhelm him. There is no doubt that for James, the stressor is indeed a significant one, but it is his visualisation of the consequences that results in toxic stress.

In all of the above cases, we can see that each person interprets the stressor of losing their job differently. Those who assess the situation logically have a reduced risk of becoming stressed. However, those who assign to the situation a consequence which may not actually materialise are likely to get into difficulty.

The best defence against chronic stress is to challenge your interpretation of a stressor. To do this, start by writing down the stressor on a sheet of paper, and attempt to answer the key question, 'Why is this bothering me at all?' The answer to this question usually results in a chain of similar questions: 'And why is that bothering me?', and so on. Eventually, we find ourselves at the core of the problem. In the examples above:

- Mary's real 'danger' is that she will lose her boyfriend.
- Maura's 'danger' is that she is too old to get another job.
- James's 'danger' is that his family will lose their house and end up on the street.

To challenge a particular interpretation, we must fully understand it first. Once we have got to the root of the problem, we can begin to examine how accurate our interpretation is. Often, we have jumped to conclusions and made all kinds of assumptions that have no basis in reality. These narratives can take on a life of their own, and cause us to 'catastrophise' about what will happen to us. Tackling chronic stress is really about developing the skills to successfully challenge these irrational thoughts.

A light-hearted way of challenging the inaccurate interpretations we attach to stressors in our lives is to consider the following statement: 'People love to believe their own bull.' This means that we are adept not only at making up elaborate stories but also at convincing ourselves they are true!

To challenge this problem, we must attempt to prove that our visualisation is going to come true. This step involves brutal honesty, otherwise we will continue to fool ourselves and thwart our journey to recovery. More often than not, people realise that what they believe to be a real danger is in fact an imagined one.

For example, if Maura challenges her belief that she is too old to get another job, she will realise that she has no evidence for this. She has never been in this situation before. She has not yet applied for any jobs, and not even considered seeking retraining. While getting a new job may be difficult, all the negative consequences she has anticipated may never arise.

Can James prove that his family will lose their home? Has he considered restructuring his mortgage repayments or using his redundancy money to ease the pressure?

John's approach to challenging his interpretation will be quite different from those of the others. He was most bothered about the fact that his employers could not see how important and valuable he was to the company. He was heading into a period of toxic stress as a result of his outrage and frustration at being let go. For John to challenge his interpretation, he must first work out what is really bothering him – that his employers did not appreciate him – and then be honest in challenging this. Was he really invaluable to the company? Did he fully understand the difficulties facing the company and what their restructuring plans involved? Could he prove whether his being let go made any significant difference? Or did John just 'believe his own bull'?

But what can we say to those who are presented with situations in which, no matter how we look at them, disaster seems to be lurking? Many who are in these situations are facing such a reality and can argue that no matter how they view the trigger facing them, it is impossible to find a 'silver lining'.

The reality is that challenging the 'A' in such situations is usually a waste of time. How can we say to a person with a young family about to be evicted by a heartless, uncaring financial institution, 'Don't worry, it will all work out for the best'? Or say to somebody who has just been let go from a job and has little prospect of getting another one any time soon, 'Don't worry, things will work out – just stay positive'? Or to say to a hard-working self-employed person who has done everything in his power, including dipping into his hard-earned savings, to try to hold on to the jobs of the six people he is employing, 'Don't worry, just hang in there and everything will work out'?

For thousands of people in Ireland, these scenarios are a reality, and no amount of 'gloss' is going to change things. In such cases, challenging the validity of a stressor may seem pointless and almost an insult to their common sense. But we Irish are, as a people, incredibly resilient, and we have to come up with survival strategies for such situations. That is where challenging our underlying belief systems (particularly the ones which suggest we will not be able to cope or survive!) and the resulting negative behaviours will prove useful. A pragmatic or realistic approach can often make matters less stressful.

But there are many situations where the stressor is neither acute nor destructive. In these cases, it is our mental view of the potential problems that underlies our distress. With these provisos in mind, and having learned the importance of understanding and challenging our interpretation of stress-ors, let's examine the unhealthy beliefs and demands that often underlie them.

# STEP FOUR
# CHALLENGING UNHEALTHY BELIEFS
# AND DEMANDS

In the last section, we learnt that how we interpret events greatly influences how we deal with them. But what underlies the differences in the way each of us evaluates the stressors in question? How we interpret stressors and the resulting emotional and behavioural consequences depends greatly on our underlying beliefs, or the 'lens' through which we view life. These, as we have seen, include our thoughts and attitudes, the meaning we attach to internal and external events in our lives, and the demands on ourselves, the world and others. Most of us are unrealistic about the demands we make on ourselves, others and the world in general. These demands become problematic when they are not met. Just as we learned to evaluate and challenge our interpretation of stressors in the last section, we can also analyse:

- the role played by our personal belief system in analysing stressors
- the resulting demands we make of ourselves
- how to challenge these demands

Only through understanding ourselves and how we think can we make serious changes to our lives and rid ourselves of chronic stress. Most cases of chronic stress centre on a particular scenario: a demand that things turn out a certain way, a perception that we will not be able to cope if they don't, and a period of being self-critical when and if this happens. We must learn to understand and challenge these unrealistic beliefs and demands. Dr Bill achieves this in the following examples:

## 'He Just Can't Leave Me!'

Sara has become extremely stressed, hurt and anxious following the sudden decision by her long-standing boyfriend, Ian, to leave her. She decides, after six months of hell, to visit Dr Bill. It is clear that she is struggling to come to terms with the situation; he decides to do an 'ABC' with her. Here we will deal only with the 'A' and 'B' that they agree on and see how she learns to challenge them.

A    Activating Event:
- Trigger: the breakdown of her relationship
- Inference/Danger: She will never again be able to find somebody she can love and trust to the same degree as she did Ian; as a result, she will end up alone.

B    Belief/Demands: They identify three unhealthy beliefs/demands which are at the heart of Sara's distress and which are leading to most of her symptoms: Ian should not have left her; she must not be left alone, as she will not be able to cope (in my experience, this is one of the most common demands we make as human beings); she is a failure because she was unable to maintain the relationship.

Dr Bill moves on to show her how to challenge the above unhealthy beliefs and demands. He explains a set of ideas known as the 'Big MACS', and how he and she will use them to challenge her demand. He then challenges her beliefs as follows:

M stands for MUST: Dr Bill explains that people who suffer from stress and anxiety live in the 'Land of Must', using absolute terms like 'ought', 'should' and 'must' to demand that things be a certain way.

He explains that when we talk about life in this way, we are really demanding one of four things: certainty, order, security or perfection. Sara realises that her demand that Ian should not have left her was an unrealistic and unfair demand. As Dr Bill explained, there was no law that stated that Ian – or indeed any partner – must stay in a relationship with her. She sought a level of control over his feelings and actions that was unhealthy and unrealistic. While it would have been preferable for her if Ian had agreed to stay in the relationship, there were many factors outside of her control – namely his feelings and plans for the future – which conflicted with their relationship. They agree that this demand was a burden on her, and that she would feel much better if she accepted his decision. Sara also realises that her demand for certainty that she never be left on her own is unreasonable and unhealthy – albeit understandable.

A stands for AWFUL: Dr Bill goes on to explain that many people who suffer from stress and anxiety imagine the worst-case scenario, which is often catastrophic. They focus on the small chance that something will go wrong, rather than the more likely scenario that it won't. Sara immediately accepts this, admitting: 'I spend so much time worrying about all kinds of things that never come to fruition.' They agree that she has absolutely no proof that just because Ian left her, she would never meet anyone else and would definitely end up on her own.

C stands for CAN'T STAND IT: This is common among those suffering from stress and anxiety. Sara doesn't think she can cope with being on her own. Dr Bill challenges this belief, pointing out that she has coped with far worse situations in her life.

S stands for SELF/OTHER RATING: This lies at the root of stress, anxiety and indeed depression. It involves judging ourselves and taking on board the judgements of others. 'How would you have rated yourself before Ian left you, on a scale of one to a hundred,' Dr Bill asks. Sara replies that in general she would rate herself quite highly, probably around eighty. Her doctor draws a scale and marks her rating on it. 'And where do you feel others would have rated you?' he asks. Sara replies: 'Around the same!' He added this to the scale. 'And since Ian left you, where would you rate yourself?' he asked. Sara replies that she would drop her rating down to ten. Dr Bill marks this in too. Dr Bill then asks: 'And how do you feel other people would rate you, because he left?' Sara says: 'About ten.'

'Now a more important question,' Dr Bill continues. 'Can we really rate a person?' On reflection, Sara agrees that we cannot do this, as we are too complex.

Dr Bill then summarises the progress they have made in challenging her beliefs/demands:

- She had been looking for complete certainty that Ian would not leave her. In practice, it is neither possible nor healthy to want to control another human being. So it was better to replace the word 'must' with 'prefer'.
- This demand was a burden on her, and dropping it would help her feel better.
- She was seeking complete security in her life, and this is not possible.
- She had been imagining the worst in assuming that she would be left on her own, without any proof to confirm this.
- She assumed that she would not be able to cope on her own. In fact, she would learn to cope, even if this proved to be difficult.
- She was criticising herself and assuming that others would do likewise.

### 'She Must Get Better!'

Sue has a particularly close relationship with her sister Maeve, who has developed breast cancer and subsequently struggled through surgery, radiotherapy and chemotherapy. Sue herself has become increasingly distressed, and begins to show all the symptoms of toxic stress. Her family encourages her to see Dr Bill. Together, they analyse the problem and come up with the following 'A' and 'B':

A  Activating Event:
- Trigger: her sister's illness
- Inference/Danger: Maeve may die as a result of her illness; if Maeve does die, Sue will not be able to cope.

B  Belief/Demands: Maeve must not die.

Dr Bill convinces Sue that the best way to deal with her stress is to learn how to challenge this demand. He explains the concepts behind the 'Big MACS', and together they come up with the following:

MUST: He challenges Sue's need for complete certainty that Maeve will not die, as there was no such certainty in life. She could not control how her sister would react to a particular cancer. The variables involved, such as her sister's innate ability to fight cancer, the aggressiveness of the cancer itself, and her sister's reactions to the various therapies, were all out of Sue's control. It would of course be preferable if her sister were to survive, but *demanding* that she would survive is unrealistic.

AWFUL: Dr Bill challenges Sue's assumption that the worst will happen. In fact, Maeve might respond to treatment and make a full recovery.

CAN'T STAND IT: Dr Bill challenges Sue's belief that she would not be able to cope if her sister died. Although it would be painful and difficult, she would cope with it.

### 'She Must Stop Picking On Me!'

Pat is working in a large, impersonal organisation. Nine months previously, he had been reallocated to work in another department. His new boss, Pauline, seems to think that he was not suited to the department and she finds fault with every aspect of his work. He is finding the situation intolerable. He begins to demonstrate all the signs of chronic stress and eventually goes to see Dr Bill. They review the problem together and come up with the following 'A' and 'B':

A   Activating Event:
- Trigger: his boss giving him unachievable deadlines and unmanageable workloads
- Inference/Danger: He is being picked on; he will eventually be fired.

B   Belief/Demands: They identify some key unhealthy beliefs/demands which are at the heart of Pat's distress and which are leading to most of his symptoms: He must make his boss like him; if she does not, he will not be able to cope; he must not lose his job; he is a failure because he doesn't stand up for himself.

Dr Bill encourages him to challenge these unhealthy demands. He explains the concepts behind the 'Big MACS', and together they come up with the following:

MUST: Dr Bill challenges Pat's demand that his boss must like him. He has to appreciate that he cannot control the thoughts and behaviour of another person. Dr Bill also challenges Pat's demand for complete certainty that he would not lose his job. This is a particularly unreasonable demand in the current economic climate. While it would be better if his boss treated him with more respect, ultimately he cannot control her.

AWFUL: Dr Bill challenges Pat's assumption that the worst would inevitably happen. For example, has he any proof that his boss is trying to get him fired?

CAN'T STAND IT: In particular, Dr Bill challenges Pat's belief that he would not be able to cope if his boss did not cease her harassment, or if he actually lost his job. He would find a way of coping – both for himself and for his family.

SELF/OTHER RATING: Finally, Dr Bill challenges Pat's statement that he is a failure.

### 'I Can't Cope With His Drinking!'

Anne has been highly stressed for the previous two years as she struggles to cope with her husband Joe's drinking. His drinking has increased significantly after he lost his job a year ago. In the beginning, she had assumed he was just trying to cope with his redundancy, but it became clear that he had become addicted to alcohol. She is at the end of her tether, with unpaid bills mounting up, constant arguments, and no obvious way out of her dilemma: the couple have a substantial joint mortgage in both of their names. Finally, her sister persuades her to go for help, and she arrives into the GP's surgery to see Dr Bill. Dr Bill quickly identifies several warning signs of toxic stress; the fact that her mother died of cancer at a young age was of particular concern to him. Together with Anne, he examines the problem, and they come up with the following 'A' and 'B':

A   Activating Event:
- Trigger: Joe's drinking patterns
- Inference/Danger: Joe's drinking is destroying her life; they will end up losing their home if he does not stop; he will eventually die from his addiction; she will have a mental breakdown; she feels trapped, as separation is not financially viable for her.

B   Belief/Demands: They identify the unhealthy beliefs/ demands which are at the heart of her distress and are leading to most of her symptoms: Her husband Joe must stop drinking; they must not lose their home; she is a failure because she cannot stop him drinking.

Dr Bill then encourages her to challenge these unhealthy demands. He explains the concepts behind the 'Big MACS', and together they come up with the following:

MUST: He challenges Anne's demand that her husband must stop drinking. She could not control this. While she considered Joe's drinking to be a problem for her, he would not change until it became a problem for him. It would be better if Joe stopped drinking, but it would take either ill health or financial ruin to bring him to his senses. Until then, matters are out of her control. He also advises her to attend Al-Anon, a self-help group where other spouses of alcoholics can help her develop an insight into how to deal with his drinking problem.

AWFUL: He challenges her assumption that the worst will inevitably happen.

It is possible that they will lose their home because of how much money Joe spends on alcohol, but very few judges would throw a family out onto the street in such a situation.

CAN'T STAND IT: He challenges Anne's belief that she would not be able to cope if her husband does not stop drinking. Although it would be difficult, she would still be able to cope.

SELF/OTHER RATING: Finally, he challenges her statement that she is a failure. She reassures him that she is doing her best in a seemingly impossible situation.

### 'He Must Not Take His Own Life!'

Joan has lived under a state of unrelenting stress as a result of her son Peter. Peter's best friend Mike took his own life two years previously. This has proven to be too much for Peter, who was let go from his apprenticeship at around the same time. He became withdrawn and refused to discuss either his own situation or his friend's death. Now everyone in the house lives in a constant state of apprehension that he will follow in his friend's footsteps.

Joan has always had a special relationship with Peter and is particularly stressed by his situation: she has lost weight and spends every waking minute checking on his whereabouts. This starts to wear her down. She eventually bows to family pressure and goes to see Dr Bill. He identifies that Joan is suffering from chronic stress and notes that there is a strong family history of depression: Joan's aunt took her own life due to depression. They review the problem and come up with the following 'A' and 'B':

A   Activating Event:
- Trigger: the death by suicide of her son's best friend
- Inference / Danger: Peter is withdrawing from social life; he has been seriously affected by the suicide of his best friend; he may have become depressed, and as a result may decide to take his own life.

B  Belief/Demands: They identify the following unhealthy beliefs and demands: Peter must not decide to take his own life; if he does commit
suicide, she will not be able to cope and will be a complete failure.

Dr Bill encourages her to challenge these unhealthy demands. He explains the
concepts behind the 'Big MACS', and together they come up with the following:

MUST: He challenges her demand that Peter must not take his own life. She
cannot control his thoughts or behaviour. She should take some practical steps
to get him the help he needs, but she can never be completely certain that
events might not spiral out of control due to factors beyond her control. She
has to accept that there will always be a slim chance that Peter will take his own
life. If she does not accept this, she will be doomed to years of overwhelming
anxiety.

AWFUL: He challenges her assumption that the worst would inevitably
happen, and her visualisation of Peter in a coffin following such an incident.
Was it not equally possible that her son might come for help? Did she have any
proof that her visualisation would come true? If not, was she helping herself
by spending days worrying about something that may never actually occur?

CAN'T STAND IT: He challenges her belief that she would not be able to cope
if her son died by suicide. While it would be extremely difficult, she would
cope with it, because of her responsibilities towards the other members of the
family.

SELF/OTHER RATING: Lastly, Dr Bill challenges her statement that she is a
failure. Almost every mother and father who exists in the nightmare world of
having a family member die by suicide rates themselves as absolute failures in
the immediate aftermath of the death. This can lead to a lifetime of suffering.
Unless they can accept that no matter what happens in life they can only do
their best, this situation will not change. In relation to her son, all she can do
in the current situation is 'hang on in there' with him. She cannot control what

might happen and must accept that, no matter what actually happens, she has done her best.

## 'They Must Like Me!'

David has become extremely stressed and anxious over the last year. His problems began when he started to date Delia, a girl from a very wealthy background. In the beginning, he was able to ignore the fact that her parents were extremely disapproving of the relationship, taking the view that he did not come from 'the right stock'. The situation came to a head when they got engaged and set a date for the wedding. Delia is now caught in a tug of war between her family and David. David himself has become stressed, as he began to feel that he was not good enough for her and worried that he was causing her distress because of her family's position. He feels trapped between his love for his fiancée and the pressure he feels to become someone he is not.

Due to the stress, his health deteriorates and he begins to consider breaking off the relationship. Finally, a major bout of shingles, triggered, he believes, by the stress, prompts him to visit Dr Bill, and they discuss the problem. Dr Bill treats his shingles but tells David that he will have to deal with his stress in order to avoid risking further health consequences. They discuss the situation and come up with the following 'A' and 'B':

A   Activating Event:
- Trigger: his engagement to Delia
- Inference/Danger: Delia's family considers David to be not 'good enough' for her; he feels inferior; he may end up coming between Delia and her family; Delia may side with her family and end the relationship.

B   Belief/Demands: They identify the following unhealthy beliefs and demands: Delia's family must accept him as being good enough for their daughter; Delia must not leave him; if they do reject him, he will feel that he is a complete failure.

Dr Bill encourages him to challenge these unhealthy demands. He explains the concepts behind the 'Big MACS', and together they come up with the following:

MUST: He challenges David's demand that his new in-laws must accept him into their family and appreciate him. David needs to accept that he does not have this level of control over anyone. He also challenges David's demand for complete certainty that Delia not leave him if her parents do not accept him. It would of course be better if they stayed together, and he should do everything in his power to achieve this aim, but he has no right to insist on how another person feels or behaves.

AWFUL: He challenges David's assumption that Delia will leave him by pointing out that David has no proof that this will in fact happen.

CAN'T STAND IT: He challenges David's belief that he would not be able to cope if Delia left him. It would be difficult for him to cope, but he would manage because it would be in his own interests to do so.

SELF/OTHER RATING: Finally, he challenges David's statement that he is a failure if Delia's family reject him.

### 'I Have to Find the Money!'

Bertha has been under persistent stress since she was put on a three-day week at work. She has always been a 'spend today, pay tomorrow' person and has reached the limit on her credit card. Her bank has issued her with a final warning, and the debt collectors are due to arrive within weeks. She is not sleeping or eating, is losing weight and is getting constant mouth ulcers as a result of the stress she is under. She is arguing with her boyfriend and continuously ringing up her best friend looking for advice. As her physical health begins to decline, those close to her convince her to attend Dr Bill for help. He is concerned about her physical health and initially recommends that she takes vitamin supplements, and gets thirty minutes of brisk exercise each day. Together, they come up with the following 'A' and 'B':

A   Activating Event:
- Trigger: the upcoming visit of the debt collectors
- Inference/Danger: She will not be able to come up with the money and will lose most of her possessions; others close to her will find out that she is in debt; she will not be able to cope with the subsequent fallout.

B   Belief/Demands: They identify the following unhealthy beliefs and demands: Bertha must be able to find the money to pay off the debt collectors; she, and those around her, will think she is a complete failure.

Dr Bill encourages her to challenge these unhealthy demands. He explains the concepts behind the 'Big MACS', and together they come up with the following:

MUST: He challenges her demand that she must be able to find the money to pay off her debts. She is looking for complete certainty that she will be able to pay them off, when in reality this is not possible. This is putting intolerable stress on her; she can only do her best. Perhaps she should consider attending MABS (the Money Advice and Budgeting Service), where she could seek advice on how to restructure her financial affairs. While her debts are a significant stressor in her life, it is not inevitable that disaster will follow!

AWFUL: He challenges her assumption that the worst will inevitably happen: that all her valuables will be repossessed. She has no proof that this will happen.

CAN'T STAND IT: He challenges Bertha's belief that she would not be able to cope if the debt collectors took all her possessions.

SELF/OTHER RATING: Finally, he challenges her statement that she is a failure and encourages her to make a distinction between her behaviour and who she is as a person.

### 'I Have To Get Better!'
Paul has been extremely stressed for the previous year. He experienced major

back problems following an accident and has been out of work ever since. As his debts began to mount and pressure from work increased, Paul was showing all the signs of toxic stress. His partner was aware that Paul has a family history of premature death due to heart disease, and became increasingly worried. She finally persuades him to go for help to deal with his stress issues. He goes to see Dr Bill and agrees that he is at risk physically and emotionally. Paul agrees to do some work on the issue, and together they come up with the following 'A' and 'B':

A   Activating Event:
- Trigger: Paul's back problems
- Inference/Danger: He is never going to get better; he will be let go from his job; he will be unable to find another job; he will be unable to look after his family financially; he dreads receiving letters from the bank; he could lose his house.

B   Belief/Demands: They identify the following unhealthy beliefs and demands: His back problem must get better; if he cannot get better and look after his family financially, he is a complete failure.

Dr Bill encourages him to challenge unhealthy demands. He explains the concepts behind the 'Big MACS', and together they come up with the following:

MUST: Dr Bill challenges Paul's demand that he must get better. Aside from doing what his specialist advised him to, he has no control over this. He was looking for complete certainty that he would get better, and this is not possible. He also had to accept that he was not responsible for the accident in question; rather, he had been the innocent victim of it.

AWFUL: He challenges Paul's assumption that the worst would inevitably happen: he would lose his job and be unable to find another one. He had no proof that this would be the case, and was wasting a lot of time and energy worrying about it.

CAN'T STAND IT: He challenges Paul's belief that he would not be able to cope if he lost his job. Although it would be difficult for him to cope, it would be in his own interest, and in the interest of his family, for him to do so.

SELF/OTHER RATING: Finally, Dr Bill challenges Paul's statement that he would be a failure if he lost his job as a result of his back problems. How could losing his job make him a weakling and of no value? He had to accept that he was a special person in himself, just like all the people he came in contact with – with faults and failings, strengths and weaknesses, all combining to make him who he is.

What all the above examples show us is that we often end up making impossible demands on ourselves and holding on to unhealthy beliefs. These lead to the negative emotional, physical and behavioural phenomena which produce toxic stress. Challenging these beliefs is the key to recovering.

# STEP FIVE
# CHALLENGING THE EMOTIONAL
# AND BEHAVIOURAL CONSEQUENCES
# OF STRESS

Most of us only recognise chronic stress and seek help for it once we experience the negative consequences arising from our unhealthy beliefs and demands. These consequences include emotional, physical and behavioural responses that need to be understood and, where appropriate, challenged.

## The Emotional Consequences of Chronic Stress

The four most common emotional consequences of our unhealthy demands and beliefs are:

- ANXIETY: Persistent feelings of worry and fear, giving rise to physical symptoms
- DEPRESSION: Persistent feelings of low mood, which often follow periods of prolonged anxiety. As with anxiety, these are often accompanied by physical symptoms
- LOW FRUSTRATION TOLERANCE (DISTURBANCE ANXIETY): Annoyance or irritation that the world will not change to suit us. This too is usually associated with physical symptoms
- ANGER: Persistent feelings of extreme annoyance, at oneself or others

Anxiety is associated with increased adrenalin, and depression with increased adrenalin and glucocortisol; the latter in particular leads to an increased risk of suicide. Low frustration tolerance and anger are more associated with noradrenalin, and carry significant risks to cardiac health.

We cannot block or change our emotional responses to stress, however uncomfortable they are. We must learn to accept the way we feel. It is more helpful to challenge the underlying unhealthy demands and beliefs, and our negative behavioural responses to them.

Let's examine a few simple examples of our emotional responses to chronic stress:

- MICHAEL works in a company that is not doing well; he is unsure whether it is going to survive. This leads to a prolonged period of chronic stress. His demand is that he must be certain that he is not going to lose his job. This results in the emotion of anxiety.
- JOHN, who has a history of depression, works in the same company. He too is incredibly stressed by the thought of losing his job, and eventually his mood begins to drop. His unhealthy belief that he is worthless leads to him slipping into depression.
- NORA is another employee at the company and is also extremely stressed. She starts to experience the emotion of low frustration tolerance (disturbance anxiety) as she demands more information from management regarding the company's future.
- MELISSA is another worker at risk of being let go from the same company. Her emotion is intense anger, aimed at the bosses of the company, arising from her view that 'they should not have got us into this mess to start with!'

It would be a waste of time to try and change or challenge these emotions. Imagine saying to Michael, 'You must not be anxious,' or to Melissa, 'You must stop being angry'. We cannot simply turn emotions on or off.

# The Physical Consequences Of Chronic Stress

It is often the physical symptoms experienced as a result of our emotional responses to chronic stress that encourage us to seek help. This is because these symptoms can be so debilitating that they end up interfering with our daily lives. It is important to remember that our brain and body are connected, and that, as a result, emotions like anxiety and anger are usually associated with bodily sensations and symptoms. While most of these physical symptoms are usually not dangerous in themselves, they become a warning sign if they are present for long periods of time. In chronic stress, they are an indicator that we have high levels of noradrenalin and glucocortisol, with potentially lethal consequences. Many people reading this may not think they are suffering from toxic stress, but may identify with the physical symptoms that underlie it. Let's examine the main physical symptoms we may experience in response to particular emotions relevant to chronic stress.

## Anxiety
- increased heart rate
- stomach in knots
- muscle tension
- headaches
- shortness of breath
- sweating
- feeling faint
- fatigue
- irritable bowel
- sleep difficulty
- lack of libido
- muscle pains

## Depression
- exhaustion

- sleep difficulties
- poor appetite
- lack of libido

## Low Frustration Tolerance and Anger

- increased heart rate
- shallow breathing
- muscle tension
- fatigue
- lack of libido
- headaches

As with the emotional consequences of chronic stress, it is impossible try to stop all these physical symptoms, as they are the natural bodily responses to our emotions. It is extremely useful to identify them, however, as they are markers of the underlying hormonal barrages unleashed in toxic stress. What we *can* do is apply lifestyle changes and therapies to dampen down these physical responses.

# The Behavioural Consequences of Chronic Stress

While we cannot challenge either our emotional or physical responses to stress, we can challenge our behavioural responses to it. In fact, how we behave in response to stress determines to a large extent how much at risk we are to the consequences of stress. Our behavioural responses to stress usually mirror the unhealthy demands and beliefs we are making!

We can divide behavioural responses to stress into four categories:

- Avoidant behaviour
- Safety behaviour
- Aggressive behaviour
- Toxic lifestyle behaviour

## Avoidant Behaviour

This is common in those suffering from anxiety or depression due to chronic stress. In order to avoid the unpleasant physical responses, many try and avoid thinking about or dealing with the problem in question. In other cases, they avoid starting or finishing tasks due to fatigue. They may also avoid planning for the future. Examples of this are avoiding looking for a new job following redundancy, avoiding contacting the bank when a mortgage repayment is missed, or avoiding relationship counselling when one's relationship is in difficulties. This behaviour simply exacerbates the stress, and leads to further anxiety and low mood.

## Safety Behaviour

This is also common in those suffering from anxiety or depression due to chronic stress. One way of coping with stress is to seek safety and security. A typical example would be where a person fears they are about to lose their job and constantly seeks reassurance from the company, or a person who is in financial difficulty spending more and more time going over bank statements.

## Aggressive Behaviour

This is common in those who respond to chronic stress with anger or low frustration tolerance. Aggression leads a person to express uncomfortable emotions in a physical manner. Examples of this would be road rage, explosive arguments over minor problems in the home, and an unwarranted outburst from an irate boss. Where alcohol is involved, these outbursts can become dangerously violent. Those who show aggressive behavioural patterns seem to be particularly susceptible to the health risks of toxic stress.

## Toxic Lifestyle Behaviours

These are the most unrecognised consequences of toxic stress. While the physiological consequences of chronic stress are incredibly damaging to physical and mental health, the lifestyle behaviours can be just as problematic. When we experience many of the emotions and physical symptoms of stress, we often engage in the following behaviours:

- EATING UNHEALTHILY – we stop cooking properly and eating fresh fruit and vegetables, instead eating processed food, missing key meals such as breakfast, and becoming deficient in key vitamins and nutrients
- STOPPING EXERCISING on a daily basis and spending too much time watching TV
- As a result, developing OBESITY, which brings with it a host of negative consequences, such as diabetes, heart disease, high blood pressure and back problems
- DRINKING ALCOHOL to excess
- USING ILLEGAL DRUGS such as cocaine or hash to cope, running the risk of serious consequences for physical and mental health
- SMOKING MORE, increasing the risk of heart disease and lung cancer
- Spending too much time on the INTERNET AND SOCIAL NETWORK-ING SITES, as well as gambling and gaming online

While it would be a waste of time to challenge the physical symptoms or emotions underlying toxic stress, it is possible to challenge unhealthy behaviours. Here are some examples of Dr Bill changing such patterns of behaviour.

### 'I Can't Stop Coughing!'

Jim goes to see Dr Bill with persistent coughing for the previous six months. He is a forty-four-year-old business executive who has spent the previous year in a state of constant stress due to difficulties in collecting money owed by clients. He is under pressure from his superiors to deliver results and has become highly anxious, leading to a range of unhealthy behaviours. He is staying late at work and becoming physically and mentally exhausted. He is eating junk food and drinking too much. As a result, he is sleeping poorly and has lost all interest in sex. He is also smoking up to forty cigarettes a day, and constantly drinking coffee. Following a medical examination, he is diagnosed with chronic bronchitis due to smoking. Jim's own father died from lung cancer; while Dr Bill reassures Jim that he does not suffer from this, his lifestyle requires dramatic changes if he is to avoid a similar fate. He challenges Jim's behaviour by making the following points:

- Jim is using cigarettes and coffee as a coping mechanism to deal with his stress. These habits are increasing his risk of cancer and heart disease.
- Jim's diet and lack of exercise are making him heavier and putting him at risk of diabetes and heart disease.
- His excessive alcohol intake could develop into a serious problem.
- His lifestyle is putting his job in jeopardy because of his increased risk of developing serious illness.

Jim implements Dr Bill's recommendations and six months later reports that he feels like a new man. He weighs a stone less, has stopped smoking, exercises for thirty minutes a day, and has a far healthier diet. He is spending less time working late and more time with his family. To his great surprise, he is performing better at work and is much less anxious about his future.

### 'I Just Can't Believe That it Was Me That Suffered a Heart Attack!'

Paul arrives in to see Dr Bill following a serious heart attack, after which he had to be resuscitated. At work, he is one of the firm's leading performers. He is just forty-two and is still shocked that he suffered a heart attack. He says he was 'too busy' for such an inconvenience! Paul fits into the type A personality category (competitive, aggressive, impulsive, impatient and goal-orientated). He had been under severe stress over the last five years while the company was being restructured. He is in charge of the redundancies, with fifty employees having been let go so far. He is renowned as being difficult to work with, with a tendency for making outbursts when he doesn't get his way. He separated from his partner two years previously, as she couldn't cope with his temper or his drinking binges. He is eating poorly and has put on several stone in weight. His main weekly exercise of playing football is more of an excuse for aggression rather than being done with the aim of getting fit. Despite this, and his heavy smoking, he is rarely sick; indeed, he views being sick as a form of weakness. He collapsed during a Monday-night football session, and only survived because a defibrillator was available nearby. Paul is quite fixed in relation to his thinking and behaviour, and tells Dr Bill that he is too busy to change his lifestyle. Dr Bill explains the links between stress, unhealthy behaviours, heart disease and premature death. Paul admits that he would prefer to stay alive, and asks for some advice. Dr Bill recommends that Paul do the following:

- stop smoking
- reduce his alcohol intake
- start working with a dietician to manage his weight
- take thirty minutes of brisk exercise every day
- temper his aggressive outbursts
- attend classes in mindfulness
- work with Dr Bill on the demands behind his aggressive behaviour

Paul initially accepted Dr Bill's challenge but had regressed to his usual behaviour within three months, coming to the conclusion that Dr Bill was a 'quack' and didn't know what he was talking about. Paul died six months later from a massive heart attack. Not everybody wants to give up their unhealthy thinking patterns and lifestyle behaviours.

## 'I Just Couldn't Go On!'

Maura is referred to Dr Bill by her own doctor following a suicide attempt. She is accompanied by her partner, having spent more than a week on a life-support machine. She has found herself in a financial nightmare: she and her partner have both lost their jobs and are being hounded by the banks because of debts and mortgage arrears. The stress of this persisted for more than a year, and resulted in constant rows between her and her partner. She smoked constantly and stopped eating, with her family and friends becoming worried about her weight loss. Her anxiety eventually led to low mood, and she had become increasingly withdrawn and apathetic. Eventually, her partner was unable to cope with what he perceived as her apparent rejection of him, and her general behaviour, and moved out to stay with his family.

Maura became increasingly consumed by toxic stress, her mood hit rock bottom, and she felt she couldn't go on. She thought the world would be a better place without her and even checked her life assurance to see how much her partner would get in the event of her death. She went from shop to shop and built up a potentially lethal supply of paracetamol. She took out the bottle of wine and consumed all the tablets, eventually becoming comatose. Fortunately, her sister, who had been worried about her, called round. When Maura finally regained consciousness ten days later, she was filled with a mixture of emotions: guilt at what she had done, and sadness that she had not been successful. Her partner is now back by her side – upset with himself that he had not recognised how depressed she was. She accepts Dr Bill's help in trying to sort out her emotional problems. Dr Bill is extremely supportive and helpful and is able to show both Maura and her partner how the prolonged period of stress had triggered her depression and how this had led to suicidal thoughts and actions.

He offers to help her deal with her depression but points out that this will involve making significant changes to her life relating to diet, supplements, exercise, and counselling and drug therapy. He goes on to challenge many of the toxic lifestyle behaviours she had developed as a result of her stress, explaining to her how they were continuing to contribute to her difficulties. They agree that Maura will make the following changes:

- stop smoking
- stop drinking alcohol until her mood has returned to normal
- eat a healthier diet and take supplements
- exercise for at least thirty minutes every day
- seek financial advice
- work out a new arrangement with the bank
- attend counselling with her partner

Both Maura and her partner agree to the above and are committed to making the necessary changes. The bank is very accommodating when they learn of her situation. Nine months on, she is back at work in a new job. She feels much better: she is not drinking alcohol or smoking, is exercising daily and is taking regular supplements. She spends some time working with Dr Bill on her negative thoughts using simple CBM/CBT concepts. She has also accepted his offer of developing mindfulness and spends fifteen minutes a day learning to be 'in the present'. A year later, she is pregnant, and the house, which was previously so full of sorrow, becomes full of joy.

There are many lessons to be learned from this story:

- Toxic stress builds up if we do not act in time. For example, Maura should have sought financial assistance much earlier.
- Chronic stress can lead to a major bout of depression.
- Stress is often worsened by poor diet, lack of exercise and increased alcohol consumption.
- Suicidal thoughts and actions are a potentially lethal but avoidable consequence of toxic stress. Acting on these thoughts can sentence those left behind to a life-time of grief.
- The earlier you come for help, the easier it will be to get on the road back to health. If you have become extremely distressed, open up to someone close to you. This step is usually the hardest to take.
- If you ever find yourself in this situation, take that first step! It may end up saving your life and preventing the destruction of the lives of those you love.

# STEP SIX
# PUTTING IT ALL TOGETHER –
# A WORKING MODEL OF TOXIC STRESS

The last few chapters have demonstrated how to identify chronic stress in our lives. They have also covered how to evaluate and challenge:

- stressors and our interpretation of them (CHALLENGING THE 'A')
- our unhealthy beliefs and the demands we place on ourselves (CHALLENGING THE 'B')
- the emotional, physical and behavioural consequences of such beliefs and demands (CHALLENGING THE 'C')

To challenge the 'A', 'B' and 'C', we must put our responses to stress into a structured model to enable us to make sense of our situation. Below are a number of examples which show this process in action, and how Dr Bill uses this model to help various people reduce their risk of developing the serious physical and psychological consequences of toxic stress.

In these examples, we are going to examine in more detail just what happens as Dr Bill assists them in using the ABC model that we have discussed in previous chapters. We are going to follow as he takes them through each step of their individual ABCs. This will help you to see just how applying it would work in practice and give you a template to cope with toxic stress in your life. They also cover many of the common causes of toxic stress that we dealt with earlier in the book.

## 'Why Am I Feeling So Constantly Wired'?

Roger a forty-year-old businessman comes to see Dr Bill with his wife Mary. He has a high-powered job in the city but is insidiously developing the symptoms of toxic stress. He has become increasingly fatigued, constantly on edge, snappy which was so unlike him and increasingly frustrated when even the slightest thing goes wrong at home or work.

Mary has become increasingly concerned. 'He is just not himself for the past year' she explains to Dr Bill. 'Normally he is quite good-humored and gets on well with the children. But over the past year, especially in past few months he has changed completely. Now he seems to be constantly complaining of minor ailments, cold sores, mouth ulcers and is also becoming quite down at times'.

Roger agreed: 'It is just not like me to be like this. I am normally quite easygoing but now find myself completely wired all the time, constantly on edge. I am even becoming one of those people I hate on the road. You know the type. They drive up your tail end and flash away till you move over to let them out. Luckily I only drive at the weekend. But even on the Tube, I feel myself overreacting to even the slightest pressure from the usual morning and evening rush'.

Dr Bill began to probe further. It became clear that Roger was going to bed late, spending increasing time on the computer or aimlessly watching TV or Netflix. He felt tired but so wired that he couldn't face lying down and trying to sleep. His fatigue had really worsened over the previous few months and he was now worried that 'there must be something physically wrong'! Dr Bill did a full physical examination and referred Roger for a complete blood screen. As he anticipated this turned out to be completely negative.

Roger became quite despondent when he was given the all clear. 'There must be something wrong,' he protested. 'I could not be feeling and behaving like this if I am physically healthy.

Dr Bill then went on to explain that he felt that Roger was suffering from the classical signs of toxic stress. This was a huge relief to him. He now at least had a name for what he was suffering from, namely 'toxic stress'. Even the name sounded right to him. 'That is exactly how I feel' he exclaimed 'so stressed out all of the time'.

Dr Bill went through the usual steps in relation to his lifestyle. He advises Roger to start exercising (which he had completely ceased to do), to improve his diet, which had reduced to non-stop coffee, minerals and chocolate, and to significantly reduce his alcohol levels, as these too had dramatically increased.

He then began to take Roger's life to pieces, looking for the missing piece driving his toxic stress. This initially proved more difficult than he imagined, for Roger was quite happily married, deeply in love with his wife, and genuinely cared for his two children, so there were no issues there. He then probed for difficulties at work. Once again it appeared that Roger was very happy at his job and quite successful and popular with customers. He was not being bullied in any form and had generally good working relationships with his colleagues. The only pressure came from the target-driven nature of the company, but he felt that was something he was used to. There were also no issues with wider family such as ageing parents or other siblings.

Finally, Dr Bill identified the problem. It related to Roger's relationship with technology, with a special emphasis on his addiction to checking and replying to his emails and Twitter account. 'And which of these is the greater problem?' he asked. Roger had no hesitation in replying that it was his obsession with emails that was the major issue. 'It starts at five in the morning and will go on till I finally fall asleep at midnight,' he admits. 'On reflection, this may be partially linked in with the customer base abroad and trying to keep them happy,' he added. He went on to explain that he felt this was essential if he was going to reach his targets.

Dr Bill decides to do an ABC on the subject with Roger to try and tease out the purpose of this obsessive behaviour. He initially explains about Rational and Irrational Beliefs, how the ABC concept would work, and how they would use this system to try and locate and deal with his Irrational Beliefs.

They decide that they would use his annual targets as the trigger.

He begins by asking Jim, 'How did you feel emotionally about having to reach these annual targets'? Roger identifies that he has become extremely anxious and also quite frustrated by them. 'And how do you feel physically when you do become anxious' asks Dr Bill.

Roger admitted to being 'constantly tired, stomach in permanent knots, muscle tension, nonstop cold sores and mouth ulcers; not to mention grinding my teeth at night and waking up with facial pain'.

Dr Bill asks him to write this down on their ABC sheet:

A  Activating Event:
• Trigger: his annual targets
• Inference/Danger:

B  Belief/Demands:

C  Consequences:
• Emotions: anxiety, frustration
• Physical reactions: fatigue, stomach in knots, tension headaches, night-time grinding, facial pains and cold sores and mouth ulcers
• Behaviour:

Dr Bill then moved on to query 'what is it about these targets that is making you feel so anxious'?

'My main fear is that I will get behind in my targets,' explains Roger.

'And what do you visualize will happen if you do fall behind with these targets'?

'This is what keeps me awake at night,' said Roger, 'because I know that the company take these targets very seriously. They reward you with bonuses if you make them, but are quite ruthless if you struggle to reach them'.

'But what do you think would happen if you didn't reach them? persisted Dr Bill.

'I hate to even think about that possibility. One of my colleagues did lose his job last year. And now that I come to think about it, that was when all of this began'.

'So, your real danger is that you might lose their job. But why would that bother you?' asked Dr Bill.

'It would be disastrous. We have a large mortgage and even at my age it is getting harder to get jobs as good as this. I might possibly be able to find something but we could end up really struggling otherwise. I could even see the house under threat'.

'So now we know why these targets are making you anxious; but what is it about them that is making you feel frustrated?' asked Dr Bill.'

'I feel that I have been with the company for so many years and have always managed to bring in good figures and keep customers happy. It just seems ridiculous that I should have to be put up with this pressure at my stage. I can see their importance for younger colleagues just beginning but not at my stage'.

Dr Bill empathized and asked him to add this information to their ABC:

A   Activating Event:
- Trigger: his annual targets
- Inference/Danger: Roger might not reach his annual targets; if this happened he might lose his job; might be unable to find a replacement; might struggle to pay mortgage; was too experienced to be asked to reach targets.

B   Belief/Demands:

C   Consequences:
- Emotions: anxiety, frustration
- Physical reactions: fatigue, stomach in knots, tension headaches, night-time grinding, facial pains and cold sores and mouth ulcers
- Behaviour:

'Let's move on to see what Irrational Belief was triggered by this situation and the inference you assigned to it' said Dr Bill. 'This usually takes the form of some absolute demand you are making about the trigger. Let's examine first what beliefs or demands were you making that resulted in you feeling anxious'.

'That is simple', answered Roger. 'I must reach my targets!'

'And how would you feel about yourself if you were unable to achieve these demands?'

'I would feel a total failure!'

'And what demand were you making that resulted in you feeling frustrated?'

Roger had to think about this but after some discussion he decided that his demand was 'that he should not have been asked to reach these targets in the first place'!

They then added this information to their ABC:

A   Activating Event:
*   Trigger: his annual targets
*   Inference/Danger: Roger might not reach his annual targets; if this happened he might lose his job; might be unable to find a replacement; might struggle to pay mortgage; was too experienced to be asked to reach targets.

B   Belief/Demands: He must reach his targets and not lose his job; if he is unable to hold on to his job, he is a failure; he should not have been asked to reach such targets in the first place.

C   Consequences:
*   Emotions: anxiety, frustration
*   Physical reactions: fatigue, stomach in knots, tension headaches, night-time grinding, facial pains and cold sores and mouth ulcers
*   Behaviour:

'So, what did you do, Roger, when you became very anxious that you would not be able to achieve these demands? It is often our behaviour, in such situations, that causes us difficulties,' asked Dr Bill.

'I know that I became increasingly focused on keeping the customers happy at all costs,' he replied.

'And what did you to try and achieve this objective?'

'I tried to stay on top of my emails no matter what else was happening in my life'.

'Can you elaborate on what you mean by this?' asked Dr Bill. 'Does this mean that you were constantly on your smart phone?'

'I became obsessed with checking it,' admitted Roger. 'It started at five am and by seven am my head was filled with the issues mentioned in the emails'.

This led to a serious discussion as to just what had been happening in Roger's life since his colleague had lost his job a year before.

He spent every waking minute on his smart phone from waking up at five am all the way through to midnight. Even at night it was charging beside him by his bed. It was constantly blipping all night long as customers contacted him from different time zones.

He admitted to spending all his time when commuting, eating his meals, even when talking to colleagues and his wife, constantly checking and rechecking his emails. He also mentioned time spent on Twitter on business matters.

By evening time, he was exhausted, spending his time mindlessly watching TV, checking his emails and Twitter whilst avoiding any form of exercise. Recently he had taken to alcohol to cope with his anxiety and frustration. All of this was causing difficulties for Mary who whilst very understanding was finding his complete inertia very frustrating. He also struggled increasingly to spend quality time with his children!

Dr Bill now felt that they had a much better handle on why Roger was getting so toxically stressed. They went ahead and added this to their ABC:

A   Activating Event:
- Trigger: his annual targets
- Inference/Danger: Roger might not reach his annual targets; if this happened, he might lose his job; might be unable to find a replacement; might struggle to pay mortgage; was too experienced to be asked to reach targets.

B   Belief/Demands: He must reach his targets and not lose his job; if he is unable to hold on to his job, he is a failure; he should not have been asked to reach such targets in the first place.

C   Consequences:
- Emotions: anxiety, frustration
- Physical reactions: fatigue, stomach in knots, tension headaches, night-time grinding, facial pains and cold sores and mouth ulcers
- Behaviour: Roger spends his time constantly checking his emails and

Twitter; does so in early morning, at meals, when travelling to work; has stopped exercising and eating healthily; stops spending quality time with children and spouse; has become quite irritable when dealing with colleagues and family; is drinking alcohol daily to cope with stress.

He then proceeds to assist Roger in challenging much of the above.

CHALLENGING THE A – they decide that they could challenge the inference that he might not reach his targets or that he would lose his job. Or indeed that he would be unable to find another job if this in fact happened. Where was his evidence for either of these two possibilities happening? But they decided it that it would be simpler and more effective to challenge his underlying unhealthy demands and beliefs.

CHALLENGING THE B – Dr Bill then convinces Roger that the best way out of his present problems is to learn how to challenge his unhealthy demands. He explains the concepts behind the big MACS and together they come up with the following:

MUST – Dr Bill firstly challenged his demand that he absolutely must not fail to reach his target or lose his job! They agree that it would be preferable if this did not happen – and they would certainly take steps to try and ensure this would be the case– but he couldn't demand it. For demanding 100% certainty that this would not happen was out of his control to deliver. This led to a discussion about the whole area of control and how impossible it was in real life to achieve it!

He also challenged Roger's demand that he should not have to put up with the discomfort of having to reach these targets at his age. Was this not just company policy? Why would Roger be treated differently to everyone else in the company? Much as he would like it to happen, the world was unfortunately not going to change to suit him!

AWFUL – Dr Bill challenged his assumption that the worst would inevitably happen. Has he any proof that his emotional visualization of what was going to take place was indeed true. Furthermore, has he any proof that the catastrophising was in fact going to happen. He explained the importance of writing down his evidence that what he was visualizing would happen. This was because when it was going on in his emotional mind, his rational or logical brain was side-lined. But when he wrote it down the latter could now be involved.

CAN'T STAND IT – Dr Bill challenged his belief that he would not be able to cope if all his fears did occur. He would cope – it would be difficult, but it would be in his own interest and especially in the interest of his family to do so.

SELF/OTHER RATING – Finally, Dr Bill challenges Roger's statement that he would be a failure if he did lose his job.

CHALLENGING THE C – they decide that he had to simply accept his emotional reactions of anxiety and frustration as normal and do nothing to change them. Similarly, in relation to his physical symptoms it was better to regard them as normal physiological responses to his emotions.

In relation to his behavioural responses, Dr Bill challenges Roger as follows:

- Was checking his emails constantly really going to assist him in reaching his targets?
- Was it not more likely that it was increasing his levels of anxiety and frustration, reducing the quality of his sleep and discouraging him from living a normal healthy life?
- Was this behaviour reducing the quality time he could spend with his family?
- Was it not leading to him taking alcohol in evenings to try and cope with his toxic stress?
- Was it not more likely that if he continued this suite of behaviours that his mental and physical health would be increasingly put at risk?
- Was his constant irritation with colleagues and family about having to achieve these targets only adding to the toxic stress symptoms he was experiencing?

Roger found the whole process really enlightening and suddenly realized just what had been going on for the previous year and the rut he had found himself in. He worked out with Dr Bill a complete overhaul of his day-to-day life. He set up clear protocols in relation to technology and his emails and Twitter accounts. His bedroom was transformed from an airline cockpit into a calm, peaceful place, designed to encourage relaxation. He ceased alcohol intake and agreed with his manager that work would be left in the office.

He also began to exercise regularly and totally transformed his unhealthy dietary habits. He also worked hard to stop demanding that the world had to change to suit him.

Six months later, he is a new man. He is no longer stressed, is sleeping normally, exercising regularly, even doing some meditation tapes. His relationships with Mary and his children have been transformed.

He has also faced toxic stress head on and in the process prevented some very serious long term physical and psychological consequences.

### 'We Do Nothing but Fight!'

Jean comes to see Dr Bill complaining of a host of symptoms: exhaustion, lack of sex drive, and impaired short-term memory and concentration. She has two children and works part-time in a call centre; she is struggling to make ends meet. Her partner Kevin finds it difficult to hold down a job, which is a cause of tension in the house. Fortunately, they are renting and do not have the added pressure of a mortgage. Nonetheless, Jean finds juggling her work with ferrying the kids to school difficult. If Kevin was not working, he had time to help, but could not contribute to the household financially, and vice versa.

As a result, she becomes very anxious and upset, and after a period where Kevin is out of work for a long time, they argue constantly, and she stops eating properly. Jean's mother observes her rapid weight loss and is convinced that she is physically ill. Following some tests carried out by Dr Bill, it becomes clear that the problem is chronic stress. She tells Dr Bill about the tense atmosphere in the house and that she and her partner (whom she still loves) did 'nothing but fight'.

Dr Bill advises Jean on her lifestyle, nutrition, exercise and alcohol consumption. Her most pressing problem is financial, due to her partner losing his job. They decide to do an 'ABC' of the problem.

Dr Bill then went on to explain the ABC concept to her and how they would use this system to try and locate and deal with her Irrational Beliefs. She is encouraged by his explanation that the best way to deal with her distress is to try and identify these beliefs and convert them into Rational Beliefs.

She gives him a typical example of when her partner returns one day to tell her that he has been let go yet again and they do the following ABC.

Dr Bill begins by asking her, 'How did you feel emotionally when this happened?' Jean is unsure of how she felt, so Dr Bill gives her a menu of emotions to pick from and she decides that she was anxious, depressed and very frustrated.

He asks her to write down this information on their ABC sheet:

A   Activating Event:
- Trigger: her partner loses his part-time job
- Inference/Danger:

B   Belief/Demands:

C   Consequences:
- Emotions: anxiety, frustration and depression
- Physical reactions:
- Behaviour:

He then asked her how she felt physically on becoming anxious and depressed. Jean explained that 'I have been constantly tired, very tense, cannot concentrate, and have lost all interest in food'. She added, 'The weight is just falling off me'. She also noted that her stomach was in constant knots and that she was grinding her teeth at night and waking up in the morning with a pain on the left side of her face. 'I am just so miserable,' she added.

Dr Bill empathized with her and explained what was going on in her body that was giving rise to these symptoms. It was a relief to her to understand that it was simply her stress system in turmoil due to a flood of stress hormones that were giving rise to her physical symptoms.

They went ahead and added this information to her ABC sheet:

A   Activating Event:
- Trigger: her partner loses his part-time job
- Inference/Danger:

B   Belief/Demands:

C   Consequences:
- Emotions: anxiety, frustration, and depression
- Physical reactions: fatigue, poor concentration, headaches, muscle tension, bowel spasms, facial pain secondary to nocturnal teeth grinding, weight loss due to loss of interest in food
- Behaviour:

Dr Bill then asked Jean, 'What was it about your partner losing his job that firstly made you feel anxious?'

She began to explain, 'My most immediate fear is that we will not have enough money to survive'.

'And why would that bother you?' he asked.

'The big worry is that we will not be able to pay the bills. I can already see them starting to build up. It is only a question of time before we fall behind in our rent repayments,' she answered. She went on to explain that her real nightmare was that they would end up evicted and homeless with nowhere to go. 'I would feel such a failure if, after everything, my children end up on the street!'

'And what was it about the situation that was making you feel so frustrated?' he asked.

'I just felt frustrated that I had to put up with this daily grind of trying to make ends meet and that Kevin was not able to contribute more financially'.

Dr Bill then asks her to add this to their ABC:

A   Activating Event:

- Trigger: her partner loses his part-time job
- Inference/Danger: that once again they will be short of money; that it will become increasingly difficult to pay their bills; that they may struggle to pay the rent and eventually be evicted; that she couldn't cope with a further period of scrimping and scraping for every penny

B   Belief/Demands:

C   Consequences:
- Emotions: anxiety, frustration and depression
- Physical reactions: fatigue, poor concentration, headaches, muscle tension, bowel spasms, facial pain secondary to nocturnal teeth grinding, weight loss due to loss of interest in food
- Behaviour:

'Let's move on to see what Irrational Belief was triggered by this situation and the danger you assigned to it,' said Dr Bill. 'This usually takes the form of some absolute demand you are making about the trigger. Let's examine first what demand you were making that was making you anxious.'

Jean, on reflection, felt her demand related to their ability to pay their bills. 'I am demanding that we must be able to pay our bills,' she replied, 'because if we can't I simply won't be able to cope.'

'So, that explains why you would feel anxious,' Dr Bill noted, 'but what did you believe about yourself that was making you feel depressed?'

Jean was quite sure about the answer to this question. 'Is that not obvious. I would feel such a failure if my children ended up on the streets!'

'And what demand were you making that was making you feel so frustrated?'

'That I should not have to put up with all this hardship and discomfort,' she replied.

'So, you had three Irrational Beliefs going on,' explained Dr Bill. 'You were demanding that you must be able to pay your bills and that if your children ended up homeless then you are a failure! You were also demanding that you should not have to put up with this discomfort.' Jean agreed and they added this information to their ABC:

A   Activating Event:
- Trigger: her partner loses his part-time job
- Inference/Danger: that once again they will be short of money; that it will become increasingly difficult to pay their bills; that they may struggle to pay the rent and eventually be evicted; that she couldn't cope with a further period of scrimping and scraping for every penny

B   Belief/Demands: They must be able to pay their bills; if they cannot, she will not be able to cope; she is a failure for not being able to look after her children; she should not have to put up with this discomfort.

C   Consequences:
- Emotions: anxiety, frustration and depression
- Physical reactions: fatigue, poor concentration, headaches, muscle tension, bowel spasms, facial pain secondary to nocturnal teeth grinding, weight loss due to loss of interest in food
- Behaviour:

'So, what did you do when you became very anxious, because of this demand? It is often our behaviour, in such situations, that causes us difficulties,' asked Dr Bill.

'Well the first thing that happened was that I stopped eating and began to lose weight' replied Jean. 'I also found myself constantly thinking about what was going to happen if we could not pay our bills and ended up ringing my mother constantly for reassurance. I couldn't sleep at night and ended up fighting constantly with Kevin over silly things. I often ended up in tears and began to isolate myself' she added.

Dr Bill nodded. 'This would be typical behaviour when we become very stressed and thus become anxious and a bit down!'

They then added this information to their ABC:

A   Activating Event:
- Trigger: her partner loses his part-time job

- Inference/Danger: They will once again be short of money; they will find it increasingly difficult to pay the bills; they will be unable to pay the rent and eventually be evicted; that she couldn't cope with a further period of scrimping and scraping for every penny.

B   Belief/Demands: They must be able to pay their bills; if they cannot, she will be unable to cope; she will have failed her children; she should not have to put up with this discomfort.

C   Consequences:
- Emotions: anxiety, frustration and depression
- Physical reactions: Fatigue, headaches, muscle tension, stomach upset, teeth grinding at night and weight loss due to loss of interest in food.
- Behaviour: ruminates constantly on her fears that they will be unable to pay their bills and will be evicted; refuses to open any post in case it is from the bank or credit card company; stops eating and can't sleep at night; rings her mother constantly, looking for assurance; and takes out her frustration on her partner by constantly fighting with him

Dr Bill proceeds to assist her in challenging these behaviours.

CHALLENGING THE A – They decide that there is little benefit in challenging her inferences and the perceived danger, as they were a realistic assessment of the situation.

CHALLENGING THE B – Dr Bill helps her challenge her demand that they must be able to pay their pay bills and that if they could not, she would be a failure and would be unable to cope. Dr Bill persuades Jean that the best way out of her problem is to learn how to challenge these unhealthy demands. He explains the concepts behind the 'Big MACS', and together they come up with the following:

MUST – Dr Bill challenges her demand that she and her partner must be able to pay their bills. He points out that she does not have complete control over this. It would be preferable if Kevin could find work, but this may not be possible; her demand for complete certainty was unhealthy.

AWFUL – He challenges Jean's assumption that the worst would inevitably happen. She does not have any proof that her emotional visualisation of what was going to take place was true. Was it not equally possible that both she and her partner might end up working again and that their financial situation might become secure once more?

CAN'T STAND IT – He challenges Jean's belief that she would not be able to cope if everything she feared came true. It would certainly be extremely difficult if her family was evicted, but she would cope.

SELF/OTHER RATING – Finally, he challenges her statement that she would be a failure and encourages her to stop rating herself, regardless of whether her financial problems are resolved.

CHALLENGING THE C – They decide that Jean must accept her emotional reactions as normal and do nothing to change them. Dr Bill also recommends exercise, yoga and mindfulness as ways in which she could deal with her emotional responses.

Similarly, in relation to her physical symptoms it was better to regard them as normal physiological responses to her emotions. Jean was a little puzzled as to the physical symptoms she was experiencing and asked Dr Bill what was causing them.

He explained to Jean about the difference between her logical and emotional brain. It was her emotional brain that oversaw her stress system and it was her stress system firing that gave rise to these physical symptoms. 'So, whenever our emotional brain senses a danger whether real or perceived it immediately activates our acute stress system which prepares us to fight or flee. It does so by activating internal nerves and by releasing our acute fear hormone adrenaline and our chronic stress hormone glucocortisol'. He explained the function of both (how the latter was making her feel so tired but wired) and how they explained many of the physical symptoms she was experiencing.

Dr Bill then introduced Jean to the importance of the amygdala. He explained how it oversaw her stress system and how it was a primitive organ whose function was to seek out danger in the environment and, if this happened, to fire. Dr Bill explained that there was in fact no actual danger to these physical symptoms, but stressed that they were extremely uncomfortable. It was this discomfort that people with Anxiety struggle to deal with. He then explored the idea with Jean of just simply learning to accept that the more she demanded they go away, the more the symptoms would increase. The more she accepted and just went with them, the more they would start to become background noise. Jean found this information extremely helpful.

They then moved on to reviewing her unhealthy behaviour patterns. This led to a very targeted discussion on what practical steps she could make to assist the situation.

Dr Bill challenged her behavioural responses:

- Continuous negative thinking about the consequences of falling into debt was not helping her deal with the problem.
- Working out a solution with her credit-card company or contacting money advisory services would be a more useful response.
- Smoking and drinking were not helping her deal with the issues.
- Better nutrition, taking supplements and getting exercise would be a better way to cope.
- Fighting with her partner was only making the situation worse.
- Seeking constant reassurance from others was not getting her anywhere.

Jean begins to implement some of these recommendations in her life. Her chronic stress, anxiety and physical symptoms start to disappear. She still struggles with money but has learned how to deal with financial issues in a positive manner. She no longer regards herself as a failure.

### 'Who Am I?'

Jim is referred to Dr Bill when his parents, to their horror, find him at home attaching a rope to the attic. He is eighteen years old. He has been in real trouble physically and mentally for the previous two years and was suffering from all the classical signs of toxic stress. He had lost weight, was quite down, was getting continuous mouth ulcers and was having difficulties with sleep, food and concentration. He was also feeling exhausted for large parts of the day. His parents had assumed that all of these things were due to the typical stress experienced when heading into exams. Jim's issues were, however, deeper and more sinister. He had always been quite shy and bookish. He had a few interactions with girls, but felt awkward and uncomfortable in their presence.

Unfortunately, this had led to a two-year period of being unmercifully mocked and bullied by a hard-core element in the school. Word was put out that he was gay, and this had a profoundly upsetting effect on Jim, who began to question his sexuality and indeed his self-esteem. He experienced continuous 'cyberbullying' in the form of nasty text messages and Facebook comments, and on one occasions found himself being filmed on a mobile phone after being 'roughed up'. He was afraid of broaching the issue at home or at school due to his fear of inviting more bullying.

He began to feel trapped, and his stress levels rose. He was already coping with the pressure of upcoming exams; it was all too much. Suicide thoughts were coming more and more. It would be for the best. Maybe then there would be some peace – for he had reached a stage where he no longer knew who he was.

His mood dropped further, and he saw no other way out. Luckily, his mother came back to the house earlier than expected, and disaster was averted.

Dr Bill spends some time with Jim and puts together all the pieces. It is clear that the lad is suffering from chronic stress and low mood. He arranges to have him assessed by the psychiatric team. The school moves in, with the help of parents, to tackle the bullies. In the meantime, they decide that it would be helpful to examine both his lifestyle and the issues that had led to the problem.

Dr Bill suggests a holistic approach of proper nutrition, daily exercise, supplements, avoiding alcohol, some counselling and, if it was felt necessary by the specialist, possibly a course of anti-depressants.

In fact, the latter is not required: Jim's mood improves by itself due to the relief of opening up about his problems, the improvement in the situation at school, and the changes in relation to nutrition, supplements, counselling and exercise. But he is still struggling with his original identity issues. He asks Dr Bill for some help.

Dr Bill decides they will do an ABC on his problems. He initially explains the ABC concept to Jim and how they would use this system to try and locate and deal with his Irrational Beliefs. He is encouraged by his explanation that the best way to deal with his distress is to try and identify these beliefs and convert them into Rational Beliefs.

They decide that his trigger was being bullied as his schoolmates thought he was gay.

Dr Bill begins by asking Jim, 'How did you feel emotionally when this happened to you?' He is unsure of how he felt so Dr Bill gives him a menu of emotions to pick from and he decides that he was both depressed and ashamed.

Dr Bill asks him to write down this information on their ABC sheet:

A   Activating Event:
- Trigger: being bullied as his schoolmates assume he is gay
- Inference/Danger:

B – Belief/Demands:

C – Consequences:
- Emotions: depression, shame
- Physical reactions:
- Behaviour:

He then asked Jim how he felt physically when he became depressed. He explained that he had become so tired, and the weight had fallen off as he lost all interest in food.

Dr Bill then moved on to query, 'What was it about your schoolmates bullying you when they assumed you were gay that caused you to feel depressed?'

Jim had to reflect on his answer. 'I began to believe that if they thought I was gay, maybe this is true' he replied.

Dr Bill tried to tease this out further. 'But did you really deep down inside feel you were gay?' he asked.

'I was always attracted to girls,' he replied, 'but became so confused when my peers began to assume the opposite was the case'.

'But why would that have led to you feeling depressed?' asked Dr Bill.

'If I couldn't even decide on my sexuality, what value was I to anyone, especially myself?'

'Did the bullying itself have any impact on you?'

'It just confirmed what I felt about myself: that I was worth nothing. Why wouldn't they pick on me?'

'And why were you feeling ashamed?' asked Dr Bill.

'I was really ashamed that they would discover that I was actually unsure of my sexuality. What would they think of me or indeed any person who was confused like I was?'

Dr Bill empathized with the difficulties Jim was going through and they added this new information to their ABC:

A   Activating Event:
- Trigger: being bullied as his schoolmates assume he is gay
- Inference/Danger: that because they think he is gay, this must make it true; he finds himself attracted to girls but very shy about relationships; that this was leading to him being very confused about his sexual identity; he felt, as a result, that he was of no value; that he could understand them picking on him: 'Wasn't he worthless anyway?'

B   Belief/Demands:

C   Consequences:
- Emotions: depression, shame
- Physical reactions: fatigue, weight loss due to loss of interest in food, difficulty with concentration

'Let's move on to see what Irrational Belief was triggered by this situation and the inference you assigned to it,' said Dr Bill. 'This usually takes the form of some absolute demand you are making about the trigger. Let's examine first what beliefs or demands were you making that resulted in you feeling depressed and ashamed.'

Jim was unsure of this but after a discussion they decided that at the heart of his difficulties lay the belief that he had felt he was worthless due to his sexual confusion. This is what led to him feeling depressed.

'But what demand were you making of yourself that led to you feeling ashamed?' asked Dr Bill.

'That they must not find out my secret,' replied Jim.

'What secret?'

'That I was confused sexually'.

'And why would this be of concern?'

'Because they would judge me'.

'And what would be their judgement?'

'That I was weak and much to be pitied'.

'So, your demand is that they must not judge you?'

'Yes' agreed Jim.


Dr Bill was now happy that they had tracked down the Irrational Beliefs that had almost led Jim into a very dark place. They added it to their ABC:

A   Activating Event:
- Trigger : being bullied as his schoolmates assume he is gay
- Inference/Danger: That because they think he is gay, this must make it true; he finds himself attracted to girls but very shy about relationships; that this was leading to him being very confused about his sexual identity; he felt, as a result, that he was of no value; that he could understand them picking on him: 'Wasn't he worthless anyway?'

B   Belief/Demands: Because of his confusion over his sexuality, he was a complete failure and of no worth; that others will find out about his confusion and judge him appropriately.

C   Consequences:
- Emotions: depression, shame
- Physical reactions: fatigue, weight loss due to loss of interest in food, difficulty with concentration

'So, what did you do Jim, when you became depressed and ashamed? It is often our behaviour, in such situations, that causes us difficulties,' asked Dr Bill.

'The first thing I did was to try to avoid my classmates as much as possible,' he replied.

'Why?'

'In case they would broach the subject and once again I would have to bear the brunt of their taunting.'

'Any other behaviours?'

'I stopped eating, struggled to sleep and avoided exercise. I also spent a lot of time on the internet but that made me even more confused. I even looked at the suicide sites as this seemed the only way out'.

'Did you consider discussing the matter with your parents?' asked Dr Bill.

'They would not have understood so I avoided this course of action,' replied Jim. 'I also fell behind in my studies – I just couldn't focus,' he added.

Dr Bill explained that this was quite typical of what we do when we become depressed or are feeling ashamed about anything and that this often led to us becoming even more stressed.

They add this to their ABC which now looks like this:

A   Activating Event:
- Trigger: being bullied, as his schoolmates assume he is gay
- Inference/Danger: That because they think he is gay, this must make it true; he finds himself attracted to girls but very shy about relationships; that this was leading to him being very confused about his sexual identity; he felt, as a result, that he was of no value; that he could understand them picking on him: 'Wasn't he worthless anyway?'

B  Belief/Demands: Because of his confusion over his sexuality, he was a complete failure and of no worth; that others will find out about his confusion and judge him appropriately.

C  Consequences:
- Emotions: depression, shame
- Physical reactions: fatigue, weight loss due to lack of interest in food, difficulty with concentration
- Behaviour: tries to avoid contact with girls due to his confusion; withdraws from contact with many of his classmates, as he is afraid they will broach the subject or mock him; stops eating, sleeping and taking exercise; spends a lot of time on the internet trying to find answers to his confusion – but none come; avoids sharing his difficulties with his parents, as he is worried that they will be upset; is falling behind in his studies, as his emotional brain is full to the brim with negative thoughts; attempts to kill himself

Dr Bill proceeds to assist him in challenging these behaviours:

CHALLENGING THE A – They decide that it is helpful to challenge his assertion that just because he is shy in his dealings with girls, he is gay. Is he not mixing up being anxious in social situations with his sexual identity?
They also agree that just because his classmates thought he was gay did not mean that he actually was. Could they look into his world? There was no evidence to back up either their, or indeed his own, fear that he was gay. In fact, everything pointed to the opposite!

CHALLENGING THE B – Dr Bill moves on and examines Jim's belief that he is worthless. Jim begins to realise that he should not rate himself or accept the rating of his schoolmates under any circumstances. He at last feels free.

CHALLENGING THE C – They move on to examine Jim's unhealthy behaviour patterns, which were worsening the situation. They decide that he will:

- exercise and eat properly
- avoid alcohol for the time being
- plan, when his exams were over, to put himself in the way of meeting girls (Dr Bill would give him some tips about social anxiety)
- open up a dialogue with his parents
- avoid negative sites on the web, which could lead him down dark roads
- stay in regular contact with his school counsellor
- report any recurrences of bullying to teachers and his parents

A year later, Jim has passed his exams and is in first year in college. He is dating a cool blonde, who falls for his gentleness and sense of humour. His former classmates are now envious! He now helps on the college website and helplines to reach other people in trouble. Jim has learned a vital message: that no matter how stressed we get, or how confused we may be about life issues, the secret is to open up and talk!

### 'I Feel So Useless!'

After working for thirty years in a local factory, Tony ends up taking an early-retirement redundancy package at the age of sixty-three. His three children have all long since left home and are now living their own lives in different parts of the country. His wife Mary had been looking forward to Tony's retirement for a number of years but, as often happens in life, things had not work out as planned.

Tony had been used to a life which was highly structured and organised. His social life had centred on his workplace and interaction with workmates; he finds retirement to be a very isolating and lonely experience.

He starts to become increasingly stressed. Mary notices that he seems fatigued and is not sleeping well. He often mopes around the house and becomes irritable and difficult to live with. He begins to drink more at home and stops frequenting old haunts where his workmates would congregrate. He also starts to develop headaches. Finally, she gets him to check his blood pressure at the local pharmacy. It is noted to be high. She finally persuades him to attend Dr Bill, who quickly gets to the core of the problem.

Having dealt with Tony's high blood pressure and reviewed his lifestyle (with a special emphasis on exercise and reducing his levels of alcohol intake), Dr Bill moves on to help Tony examine his stress issues.

Dr Bill decides that the best way to deal with this is to do an ABC on the subject with Tony to try and see why he was so distressed. He initially explains about Rational and Irrational Beliefs, how the ABC concept would work, and how they would use this system to try and locate and deal with his Irrational Beliefs.

They decide that they would use his retirement as the trigger.

Dr Bill begins by asking him, 'How did you feel emotionally about having to retire?'

Tony, on reflection, feels that he has become both ashamed and depressed since he left his job. 'And how do you feel physically when you do become depressed?' asks Dr Bill.

Tony admits to being constantly tired, struggling with sleep, appetites, libido, drive and that he had lost interest in everything. He also notes that he was struggling with concentration and memory.

Dr Bill asks him to write this down on their ABC sheet:

A   Activating Event:
• Trigger: his retirement
• Inference/Danger:

B   Belief/Demands:

C   Consequences:
• Emotions: depression, shame
• Physical reactions: significant fatigue, difficulties with sleep, drive, appetite, concentration and memory
• Behaviour:

Dr Bill then moved on to query, 'What is it about having to retire that has led to you feeling depressed?'

'I just feel that I am no longer relevant or of any value,' replied Tony.

'Can you elaborate further on what you mean by this?' asked Dr Bill.

'I felt when I was working I had a purpose, a meaning to life,' explained Tony. 'I could hold my head up high when I came home to my wife or if I met my mates'.

'Are there any other reasons that you felt so depressed?'

'All my friends were mainly centred around the workplace. I would be able to chat to them about the football and would often socialize around the weekends with them. Now all of that is gone! It was only when I left that I realized just how much my social life was bound up with them. I really miss them, miss the crack! I love Mary but you know a man also needs his mates. I also feel that I am of little value to her now. I don't bring home the wages anymore and don't feel I have much to contribute to her or indeed to anybody!'

'And how do you feel about yourself because of this?' asked Dr Bill.

'Just useless, and on occasions even feel totally worthless,' he replied.

'And what is it about your retirement that has led to you feeling ashamed?'

'It's just now, when I do meet my mates, I feel they no longer look up to me or feel that I am contributing anything any more. I feel they are quietly judging me as no longer of relevance in their lives. They don't say as much but I feel they are making their own minds up about me. After all, they are doing an important job at work whilst I am no longer achieving anything of worth in my life'!

Dr Bill empathized with him and asked him to add this information to their ABC:

A   Activating Event:
- Trigger: his retirement
- Inference/Danger: He feels that since he retired, he no longer has any value to either his wife or those around him; due to the fact that his work environment had been his main source of socialising, he feels quite isolated and alone; he feels embarrassed to meet up with former colleagues, as they are still doing an important job, while he is now only an outside observer.

B    Belief/Demands:

C    Consequences:
- Emotions: depression, shame
- Physical reactions: significant fatigue, difficulties with sleep, drive, appetite, concentration and memory
- Behaviour:


'Let's move on to see what Irrational Belief was triggered by this situation and the inference you assigned to it,' said Dr Bill. 'This usually takes the form of some absolute demand you are making about the trigger. Let's examine first what beliefs or demands were you making that resulted in you feeling depressed?'

They discussed this for a few minutes and finally Tony felt that it was his deeply held belief that because he was no longer working he was of no value or worthless.

Dr Bill agreed. 'This is what is making you feel depressed'.

They had a further discussion on the Irrational Beliefs that were triggering his shame and they decided that it was his belief that his mates would be judging him and that he must accept their judgement!

They added this to their ABC:


A    Activating Event:
- Trigger: his retirement
- Inference/Danger: He feels that since he retired, he no longer has any value to either his wife or those around him; due to the fact that his work environment had been his main source of socialising, he feels quite isolated and alone; he feels embarrassed to meet up with former colleagues, as they are still doing an important job, while he is now only an outside observer.

B    Belief/Demands: Because he is no longer working, he is of no value as a person. That his mates would judge him and he must accept their judgement.

C   Consequences:
- Emotions: depression, shame
- Physical reactions: significant fatigue, difficulties with sleep, drive, appetite, concentration and memory
- Behaviour:

'So, what did you do, Tony, when you became very depressed and ashamed as a result of these beliefs? It is often our behaviour, in such situations, that causes us difficulties,' asked Dr Bill.

'I started to isolate myself and spent hours just constantly beating myself up in my head,' he answered. 'The thoughts would just go round and round in my head'.

'That is very common,' explained Dr Bill, 'when we are feeling depressed. We call it rumination. What about other unhealthy behaviours?'

'I know I became impossible to live with, very moody and irritable. I do not know how Mary put up with me. I was also eating very poorly and stopped my normal walking routine and began to drink more than usual'.

'And what about trying to mix with your mates?' asked Dr Bill.

'I just began to totally avoid any social situations where I might meet up with them,' he answered. 'It would just have been so embarrassing!'

They added this to complete their ABC:

A   Activating Event:
- Trigger: his retirement
- Inference/Danger: He feels that since he retired, he no longer has any value to either his wife or those around him; due to the fact that his work environment had been his main source of socialising, he feels quite isolated and alone; he feels embarrassed to meet up with former colleagues, as they are still doing an important job, while he is now only an outside observer.

B   Belief/Demands: Because he is no longer working, he is of no value as a person. That his mates would judge him and he must accept their judgement.

C  Consequences:

Emotions: depression, shame

Physical reactions: significant fatigue, difficulties with sleep, drive, appetite, concentration and memory

Behaviour: ruminates constantly about the hopelessness and uselessness of his life since retirement; avoids socializing in the local haunts of his former workmates; becomes irritable and difficult to live with; eats poorly and stops taking exercise; drinks excessively at home; avoids becoming involved in any other social or sporting activities in the community; spends too much time moping around the house

Dr Bill then proceeds to assist Tony in challenging the above.

CHALLENGING THE A – They decide that they could challenge Tony's inference that he is of no value since his retirement. Could he prove that this was indeed so? Did he have any proof that his emotional visualisation, that his workmates would not want to meet him simply because he was retired, was accurate? Confronting these statements would help, but it was really his deep-seated beliefs about himself that he needed to examine.

CHALLENGING THE B – Dr Bill encourages Tony to challenge this unhealthy belief. He explains the concepts behind the 'Big MACS', and together they decide that his main problem lies in his rating of himself.

SELF/OTHER RATING – He challenges Tony's statement that he is a failure because he is no longer working. He could take a look at his behaviour to see if there were areas of his life since retirement that he could change.

CHALLENGING THE C – They decide that Tony has to accept his emotional responses to this stressor – depression – as normal. His physical symptoms are also a natural response to the way he is feeling. But Dr Bill challenges Tony's behavioural responses as follows:

- Constant rumination about his situation was not helpful: it would be better to write down the main issues, as outlined above, and challenge them.
- He would have to find a new 'passion' in his life. This might involve engaging in a wide new range of interests, to find some that appealed to him.
- He should look on this as an exciting new chapter in his life, opening up a new world of opportunities.
- In particular, he should examine the possibility of taking up some valuable voluntary work in the community, as this would have a very positive impact on his image of himself.
- He had to examine key areas like exercise, nutrition and alcohol intake in order to remain physically and mentally well during his retirement years.
- He should reconnect with his former workmates and share with them his new passions: it would be them who would finally be the envious ones!

Six months later Tony was in a new space. His mood was now back to normal. He was exercising regularly, had improved his diet and ceased alcohol at home. He had also taken to playing some pitch and putt with his old work colleagues whom he had linked back up with. He was gratified to see how delighted they were to meet up with their old and very much missed work colleague. He and Mary had also taken up dancing and had found a whole new group of friends to socialize with. He had suddenly realized that there were indeed a lot of advantages to being retired and he was now enjoying every minute of it! His toxic stress was in the past.

### 'It Brought It All Back!'

Jane is brought to see Dr Bill by her sister Maura. She had been in a state of chronic stress for over eight months but managed to keep it all hidden until finally cracking under the strain and succumbing to a bout of depression. She had taken an overdose but, luckily, had survived when she was discovered in time by Maura, who was bringing her new baby around to meet her.

Maura knew that Jane was keeping something from her but was unable to get her to reveal what was bothering her. In fact, Jane's difficulties started to arise when Maura had approached her during her pregnancy to ask her to act as godmother to her future child if all went well.

What Maura didn't know was that Jane had five years earlier found herself pregnant just as her then boyfriend walked out on her. It was a nightmare time for her as she was both financially and emotionally vulnerable. She had attended a clinic in Dublin, where it was suggested that a termination would be the best way forward, and that they could arrange for her to travel to London to have it performed. Her mind was a blur – filled with emotions of hurt and loss due to her relationship breakdown, and ashamed that her mum and dad, who are extremely conservative, would react badly to her situation. She also felt that her future career prospects would be seriously affected if the pregnancy continued.

She eventually had the termination, and on her return managed to block out what had occurred, and pick up the pieces of her life. However, her sister's innocent request triggers her emotional brain into action, and her stress levels rise further as Maura's pregnancy gets closer to term. She becomes fatigued, has difficulty sleeping, loses interest in food, and loses interest in sex with her partner, who feels rejected. Finally, her mood plummets and suicide thoughts arrive: 'I don't deserve to keep on living, and my secret can die with me.' The full weight of toxic stress arrived, putting her life at risk.

Dr Bill teases out the facts of the situation. Her mood is still extremely down; he explains that they will have to target that. He lays out a holistic approach involving exercise, nutrition, supplements and avoiding alcohol, and finally suggests a course of antidepressants – all of which she agrees to. He sees her regularly until he is happy that her mood is back to normal. As promised, he then offers to help her deal with her original stressor.

Dr Bill decides that the best way to deal with this is to do an ABC on the subject with Jane to discover why she was so distressed. He initially explains about Rational and Irrational Beliefs and how the ABC concept would work; and how they would use this system to try and locate and deal with her Irrational Beliefs.

They decide that they would use her termination as the trigger.

He begins by asking her, 'How did you feel emotionally about having had this termination?'

'I felt so guilty and so ashamed,' answered Jane, 'but eventually I became depressed'.

'And how did you feel physically when you became depressed?'

'I was so tired all the time, and really struggled with concentration, lost my appetite and the weight began to fall off me,' she answered, 'and sleep became a major problem. I would wake up in the middle of the night and found myself berating myself mercilessly!'

Dr Bill asked her to start their ABC:

A   Activating Event:
• Trigger: her termination
• Inference/Danger:

B   Belief/Demands:

C   Consequences:
• Emotions: guilt, shame, depression
• Physical reactions: fatigue, difficulties with sleep, drive, appetite, concentration and memory
• Behaviour:

Dr Bill then moved on to query, 'What is it about having had your termination that has led to you feeling so guilty?'

Jane felt the tears starting to swell up. 'I actually chose to have the termination done,' she sobbed. 'How could I have done that to my own child? I can never forgive myself for what I did!'

'Is that the main reason you feel guilty,' asked Dr Bill, 'that you ended up making a decision to terminate the life of your own child?'

'It was a combination of that decision and the fact that I allowed the clinic to persuade me that it was for the best!'

'And what was it about the termination that made you feel ashamed?' he asked.

'How could I face those close to me like friends and family if they found out that I had done something so evil? I just know what their opinion of me would be and rightly so,' she answered.

'And how do you feel about yourself Jane that you allowed the termination to go ahead?'

'I just feel awful about myself, a total failure!'

Dr Bill felt they had the bones of the problem. They added this information to their ABC:

A   Activating Event:
- Trigger: her termination
- Inference/Danger: that as a result of terminating her pregnancy, she had in effect killed her own child; that she felt very sad that she would never see the child; that she would struggle to cope if those close to her became aware of her actions; that she was upset that she had allowed herself to be convinced by the clinic to agree to the termination and could not forgive herself for making that decision; that she felt she was a failure as a result of her actions

B   Belief/Demands:

C   Consequences:
- Emotions: guilt, shame, depression
- Physical reactions: significant fatigue, difficulties with sleep, drive, appetite, concentration and memory
- Behaviour:

'Let's move on to see what Irrational Belief was triggered by this situation and the inference you assigned to it' said Dr Bill. 'This usually takes the form of some absolute demand you are making about the trigger. Let's examine first what beliefs or demands were you making that resulted in you feeling so guilty?'

'I should have made a different decision. I should not have terminated the pregnancy and taken the life of my own child,' she replied.

'And how do you feel about yourself that you did go ahead and make that decision?'

'That I am a complete failure,' she replied.

'And what were you demanding of the situation that was making you feel ashamed?' he asked.

'I was demanding that they must not find out my secret.'

'But why would this bother you?'

'Because they would judge me so harshly and I know I would have to accept their opinion as it would be justified. How could any mother do that to her child?' she replied sadly.

Dr Bill agreed that these indeed were her Irrational Beliefs and demands and they added them to their ABC:

A   Activating Event:
- Trigger: her termination
- Inference/Danger: that she felt very sad that she would never see the child; that she would struggle to cope if those close to her became aware of her actions; that she was upset that she had allowed herself to be convinced by the clinic to agree to the termination and could not forgive herself for making that decision; that she felt she was a failure as a result of her actions.

B   Belief/Demands: she should have made a different decision and not terminated her pregnancy; she was afraid that others would become aware of her secret; if they did find out, they would judge her and she must accept their judgement: she believed she was a complete failure as a person, as a result of her decision.

C   Consequences:
- Emotions: guilt, shame, depression
- Physical reactions: Fatigue, difficulties with sleep, drive, appetite, concentration and memory
- Behaviour:

'So, what did you do Jane, when you became guilty but also quite depressed and ashamed because of these beliefs? It is often our behaviour, in such situations, that causes us difficulties,' asked Dr Bill.

'I have done nothing but replaying what happened in my mind,' she answered. 'I just wish I could go back and make a different decision. I also found myself trying to block out my sister's pregnancy and upcoming labour, as they would have just consolidated the guilt which is consuming me. In fact, I try to stay away from new mums as they retrigger my guilt every time!'

'Any other negative behaviours when you were ashamed or depressed?' he asked.'

'I know I began to withdraw socially, stopped eating, lost interest in sex and above all tried to make sure nobody close to me would ever discover my secret!'

Dr Bill explained that these were all very understandable behaviours but that they would later challenge them. For the present they would add them to their ABC:

A   Activating Event:
- Trigger: her termination
- Inference/Danger: that as a result of terminating her pregnancy, she had in effect killed her own child; that she felt very sad that she would never see the child; that she would struggle to cope if those close to her became aware of her actions; that she was upset that she had allowed herself to be convinced by the clinic to agree to the termination and could not forgive herself for making that decision; that she felt she was a failure as a result of her actions

B   Belief/Demands: She should have made a different decision and not terminated her pregnancy; she was afraid that others would become aware of her secret; if they did find out, they would judge her and she must accept their judgement: she believed she was a complete failure as a person as a result of her decision.

C   Consequences:
- Emotions: guilt, shame, depression
- Physical reactions: fatigue, difficulties with sleep, drive, appetite, concentration and memory
- Behaviour: tries to hide her secret from those close to her; ruminates

constantly on what she perceives as a disastrous period of her life; stops eating and loses interest in sex; tries to avoid thinking about the arrival of her sister's new baby, as it makes her feel worse

Dr Bill proceeds to assist her in challenging these issues.

CHALLENGING THE A – They agree that there is little point in trying to deny that the termination had led to the death of her baby or that she had denied herself the possibility of seeing the child grow up. These were realities. However, she could challenge whether her emotional visualisation of how those close to her would treat her if her 'secret' came out was valid. Had she any proof that it would be as awful as she visualised? They agree that it would be better to examine her underlying beliefs and demands.

CHALLENGING THE B – Dr Bill helps her to see that her absolute demand that she should not have made the decision to go for the termination was at the heart of all her difficulties. This unhealthy demand, and her rating of herself and perceived rating by others if they learned of what she had done, were the underlying basis for her guilt, shame and depression.

Dr Bill persuades Jane that the best way to become well again is to learn how to challenge these unhealthy beliefs/demands. He explains the concepts behind the 'Big MACS', and together they come up with the following:

MUST – He explains the concept of absolute demands like 'must', 'should', 'should not', and so on. They agree that her absolute demand that she should be able to 'rewrite' her decision about going for the termination was unhealthy. Most of us in life, he explained, make decisions that at a later stage we wish we could alter. It is the nature of being human to do so. In practice, we have to go back to the circumstances surrounding the decision. She was in a very vulnerable state, emotionally due to the break-down of her relationship and the feelings of isolation and being on her own, in relation to bringing up a future child. She had to accept that although it might be preferable if she had made a different decision, the circumstances at the time created an obstacle to this.

Once she accepted that we can only make a particular decision based on the factors in play at the time, she would find it easier to accept what had happened – even if she had justifiable regrets about these things.

SELF/OTHER RATING – Dr Bill then moves on to help her challenge her rating of herself, and indeed her accepting of other people's rating if they discovered her secret.

CHALLENGING THE C – They decide that Jane must accept her emotional reactions as normal and do nothing to change them. Her physical symptoms were also normal responses to her emotions. But they decide that challenging her unhealthy behaviours would be of assistance. They decide:

- It was better to cease her constant negative reflections on what had happened and decide instead to write down her thougts in an 'ABC' manner if these thoughts persist.
- It was better to embrace the arrival of her new god-child in a positive manner, as avoiding doing so would only worsen her problems.
- That she had to continue the positive lifestyle changes already suggested in relation to exercise, and so on.
- That she had to cease trying to hide her secret and in fact might be advised to tell her sister about her past.

Within a few months, Jane's life had been completely turned around. Gone was the toxic stress that had threatened to destroy her physical and mental health. She had completely revolutionized her lifestyle with exercise and improved nutrition. She was now much more relaxed with her sister, having let her in on her secret, subsequently receiving a warm sisterly embrace and a sharing of tears. Most importantly she had really embraced the arrival of her new god-child into her life!

### 'My Life is a Living Hell!'
Mark is sent to Dr Bill after a serious suicide attempt. He had taken a drug

overdose and ended up spending a week in intensive care. He is a middle manager in a large company; he is being bullied by a new, abrasive boss who has been sent in to 'cut corners' and increase profit margins. Mark is married with two young children and is a conscientious, hard-working employee; he is usually first in and last out of the office. But for the year prior to his suicide attempt, his life was a living hell: he had begun to suffer from toxic stress. His boss mocked him in front of other staff and was impossible to please. Mark was feeling exhausted, had trouble sleeping, and could no longer concentrate properly. He developed cold sores and mouth ulcers, and lost interest in food. He started drinking more and became irritable. His mood and self-esteem began to drop. He became more withdrawn at home and spent hours late at night staring aimlessly at a computer screen or watching TV. Things came to a head when his boss began to drop hints that several jobs, including his, would have to be shed. Finally, he began to believe that there was no way out of his situation and that he was of no worth; he started to plan his suicide. Although he loved his wife and children dearly, he thought they would be better off without him around. He wrote a note for his wife explaining his decision the day before the suicide attempt. He then took an overdose.

Fortunately, his wife arrived home early, found him unconscious and got help. Following his discharge from hospital, she brought him to see Dr Bill. Mark is in two minds about the fact that he survived the suicide attempt. When he sees how much his wife cares about him, he is relieved that he was not successful. Nonetheless, his problems at work remain. Is still being alive only prolonging the agony?

Dr Bill empathises with him and is pleased that he has already been seen by a psychiatrist and prescribed an anti-depressant. He gives Mark lifestyle advice, suggesting that he take more exercise, eat properly, cease drinking alcohol and take time off work. They agree that it would be beneficial to send a report to his personnel department detailing the problems he has experienced.

Dr Bill explains how chronic stress can lead to a range of physical and emotional problems; in Mark's case, it led to depression and suicidal thoughts. If Mark is to get better, he will have to change his thinking and behaviour. Mark returns in a few weeks: by that time, his mood has improved and he is better able to concentrate.

Dr Bill decides that the best way to deal with Mark's situation is to do an ABC to discover why he was so distressed. He initially explains about Rational and Irrational Beliefs and how the ABC concept would work; and how they would use this system to try and locate and deal with is Irrational Beliefs.

They decide that they would use the suggestion that he was being bullied by his boss as the trigger.

Dr Bill begins by asking him, 'How did you feel emotionally about being bullied by your boss?'

'I felt both anxious and hurt at the beginning but eventually became quite depressed,' he replied.

'And how did you feel physically when you became depressed?'

'I was so tired all the time, and really struggled with concentration, lost my appetite and the weight began to fall off me,' he answered, 'and I had problems with sleep'.

Dr Bill asked him to start their ABC:

A   Activating Event:
- Trigger: being bullied by his boss
- Inference/Danger:

B   Belief/Demands:

C   Consequences:
- Emotions: anxiety, hurt, depression
- Physical reactions: fatigue, difficulties with sleep, drive, appetite, weight loss, concentration and memory
- Behaviour:

Dr Bill then moved on to query, 'What is it about being bullied by your boss that has led to you feeling so hurt?'

'It seemed as if no matter what I did for him I could never please him. He would praise the others but for me there was only non-stop criticism. It just wasn't fair!'

'And what was it about the situation that caused you to feel depressed?'

'I began to feel trapped in the situation and felt that I was a total failure for letting him treat me like that. I should have stood up to him more!'

They added this information to their ABC:

A    Activating Event:
* Trigger: being bullied by his boss
* Inference/Danger: He doesn't think he will ever be able to please his boss; he will never be able to cope with his job in these conditions; he feels trapped in his job;

B    Belief/Demands:

C    Consequences:
* Emotions: anxiety, hurt, depression
* Physical reactions: fatigue, difficulties with sleep, drive, appetite, weight loss, concentration and memory
* Behaviour:

'Let's move on to see what Irrational Belief was triggered by this situation and the inference you assigned to it,' said Dr Bill. 'This usually takes the form of some absolute demand you are making about the trigger. Let's examine first what beliefs or demands were you making that resulted in you feeling so hurt?'

'That is easy,' replied Mark. 'My boss should not have treated me like this'.

'And what beliefs or demands were resulting in you feeling depressed?'

'I was a failure for letting it happen'.

They add this to their ABC:

A    Activating Event:
* Trigger: being bullied by his boss
* Inference/Danger: He doesn't think he will ever be able to please his boss;

he will never be able to cope with his job in these conditions; he feels trapped in his job.

B  Belief/Demands: He is a failure; he can't cope with work anymore; his boss must not treat him in this way.

C  Consequences:
- Emotions: anxiety, hurt, depression
- Physical reactions: fatigue, difficulties with sleep, drive, appetite, weight loss, concentration and memory
- Behaviour:

'So, what did you do Mark, when you became hurt but also quite anxious and depressed and because of these beliefs? It is often our behaviour, in such situations, that causes us difficulties,' asked Dr Bill.

'I couldn't get it out of my head,' he replied. 'It was so unfair the way he treated me and I was so upset that I had let him away with it'.

'And when you became anxious?'

'I stopped accepting calls from the office and kept looking for reassurance from my wife that I would not have to return to the job. I just knew I would not be able to cope with if I was forced to. I also found myself becoming very bitter and irritable and withdrew a lot into myself'.

Dr Bill explained that although these behaviours were quite understandable, they were also adding to the toxic stress that was poisoning his life. They would challenge them later but, for the present, add them to their ABC:

A  Activating Event:
- Trigger: being bullied by his boss
- Inference/Danger: He doesn't think he will ever be able to please his boss; he will never be able to cope with his job in these conditions; he feels trapped in his job.

B  Belief/Demands: He is a failure; he can't cope with work anymore; his boss must not treat him in this way.

C   Consequences:
- Emotions: anxiety, hurt, depression
- Physical reactions: significant fatigue, difficulties with sleep, drive, appetite, weight loss, concentration and memory
- Behaviour: ruminates constantly about the way his boss is treating him; worries about how stressful work will be when he returns; avoids phone calls from work; refuses to talk things through with his wife

Dr Bill then helps Mark challenge his ABC:

CHALLENGING THE A – They decide that while they could challenge the interpretation that his boss would never treat him fairly or that he would remain trapped in this situation, it might be difficult to guarantee that these realities could be changed. It would be simpler and more effective to challenge his underlying unhealthy beliefs and demands.

CHALLENGING THE B – Dr Bill persuades him that the most effective way to deal with his problems is to learn how to challenge his unhealthy demands. He explains the concepts behind the 'Big MACS', and together they come up with the following:

MUST – Dr Bill challenges Mark's demand that his boss must change his treatment of him. He has to accept that he cannot control his boss's behaviour and that his belief that he will not be able to return to work unless things change is is fundamentally unhealthy.

AWFUL – Dr Bill challenges Mark's assumption that the worst will inevitably happen. Mark has no proof that he will lose his job.

CAN'T STAND IT – Dr Bill challenges Mark's belief that he would not be able to cope if he lost his job, or if his boss continued to bully him. In fact, he could learn to deal with both situations, if it was in his own or his family's interests to do so.

SELF/OTHER RATING – Finally, Dr Bill challenges Mark's statement that he is a failure. How could his boss treating him negatively make Mark a failure?

CHALLENGING THE C – They decide that Mark has to accept his emotional responses of hurt, anxiety and depression as normal. His physical symptoms are also a natural response to the way he is feeling. But Dr Bill challenges Mark's behavioural responses in a number of areas:

- Avoiding the company by not answering calls from them was not helping him deal with his issues.
- Discussing matters with the personnel department and other superiors would be more productive.
- Requesting a transfer was a possible option, rather than worrying about returning to the same situation.
- Not eating properly and drinking alcohol was not improving his situation.
- Improving his diet, taking supplements and exercising would be more helpful.
- Not discussing matters with his wife was holding back his recovery.
- Counselling could also be of benefit to help him deal with his situation.

Mark starts to understand what triggered his depression and works with Dr Bill to improve his situation. He releases the burden of worry he has been carrying around and becomes less anxious and depressed. He tries to resolve the situation with the company and is transferred to a new section. When his boss finds out the effects his behaviour has had on Mark, he is deeply sorry and tries to help Mark get back to work. Mark's relationship has recovered, and he has started doing charity work to help others who are in a similar situation to the one he was in. He has started exercising, eating properly, meditating and putting his personal life before work. Mark's case shows just how dangerous toxic stress can be to a person's mental health.

### 'I Can't Let Them Down!'

Hugh is the founder of a small company which employs a staff of six, who work well together. During the economic boom, the company had done very well, and the staff shared in the profits. However, after a two-year battle with toxic stress, Hugh visits Dr Bill in a terrible state: he is constantly tired, is not sleeping or eating well, feels extremely anxious, has tension headaches and panic attacks, finds it difficult to concentrate, and suffers from low mood. These symptoms started when the recession began, and orders stopped coming into the company. Exchange-rate difficulties had reduced profits, and the banks had not been very helpful. The company was struggling to survive.

By the time Hugh comes to Dr Bill, he is convinced that that he must have a serious illness: Hugh's father died from heart disease in his late fifties, and Hugh is approaching that age. He is married with three children in their teens; his wife finally convinces him to go for help when he starts to get chest pains. He has started smoking again (after having given up), and is drinking more than twice the recommended amount. He has lost weight and cannot motivate himself to exercise.

Dr Bill investigates Hugh thoroughly, and rules out any possible illnesses. His symptoms are the warning signs of toxic stress. Dr Bill explains the risks of toxic stress, especially considering his family history. They decide to tackle the problem together. First, they deal with Hugh's lifestyle. Dr Bill gives Hugh advice on diet, exercise and nutrition, and strongly challenges his smoking and alcohol consumption.

Hugh accepts his advice and begins to change his whole lifestyle. But his problems at work remain, and he asks Dr Bill for advice on how to deal with this source of stress. They agree that if he is going to get better, he has to change his thinking and behaviour

Dr Bill decides that the best way to deal with Hugh's difficulties is to do an ABC to discover the source of his distress. He initially explains about Rational and Irrational Beliefs and how the ABC concept would work; and how they would use this system to try and locate and deal with his Irrational Beliefs.

They decide that they would use the trigger of Hugh's company getting into financial difficulties.

Dr Bill begins by asking Hugh, 'How did you feel emotionally when your company began to get into difficulties?'

'I just became incredibly anxious,' Hugh replied.

'And how did you feel physically when you became so anxious?'

'I was constantly tired, my weight fell, as I had no interest in food, and I began to get a lot of tension headaches and muscle pains. I even got some chest pains which worried me even more until you and the cardiologist checked me out'.

Dr Bill then asked him to begin their ABC by putting down this information:

A   Activating Event:
•   Trigger: Hugh's company getting into financial difficulties
•   Inference/Danger:

B   Belief/Demands:

C   Consequences:
•   Emotions: anxiety
•   Physical reactions: fatigue, headaches, muscle tension, weight loss, chest pains
•   Behaviour:

Dr Bill then moved on to query, 'What is it about your company getting into financial difficulties that has led to you feeling so anxious. Or what danger were you applying to this trigger?'

'It was going to an absolute disaster. All I could visualize was the company almost lurching towards bankruptcy or going to the wall and having to let staff go to try and save it,' replied Hugh.

'And why would the latter bother you?'

'I am very close to my staff and in some cases their families. I just could not envisage having to let them down in this way'.

'And how would you feel about yourself if you did have to let them go?'

'I would feel a complete and total failure!'

Dr Bill was empathic towards his obvious distress that such an occurrence might happen and then asked him to add this to their ABC:

A   Activating Event:
*   Trigger: Hugh's company getting into financial difficulties
*   Inference/Danger: He would have to let employees go to avoid the company going into administration; he would find it very difficult to fire staff to whom he had become close; the banks were making the company's situation worse; he must not have to sack his employees; he would have a very poor opinion of himself if he had to; if he does, he will feel he has failed them.

B   Belief/Demands:

C   Consequences:
*   Emotions: anxiety
*   Physical reactions: fatigue, headaches, muscle tension, weight loss, chest pains.
*   Behaviour:

'Let's move on to see what Irrational Belief was triggered by this situation and the inference you assigned to it,' said Dr Bill. 'This usually takes the form of some absolute demand you are making about the trigger. Let's examine first what beliefs or demands you were making that resulted in you feeling so anxious.'

'I feel my main concern lay with my employees,' answered Hugh, 'so I guess my main demand was that I must not have to let any of them go'.

'And how would you feel about yourself if you did have to let them go?'

'I would feel a total failure for letting it happen!'

Dr Bill was happy with this and they added the information to their ABC:

A   Activating Event:
*   Trigger: Hugh's company getting into financial difficulties

- Inference/Danger: He would have to let employees go to avoid the company going into administration; he would find it very difficult to fire staff to whom he had become close; the banks were making the company's situation worse; he must not have to sack his employees; he would have a very poor opinion of himself if he had to; if he does, he will feel he has failed them.

B  Belief/Demands: He must not have to sack his employees; he would have a very poor opinion of himself if he had to; if he does, he will feel he is a failure.

C  Consequences:
- Emotions: anxiety
- Physical reactions: fatigue, headaches, muscle tension, weight loss, chest pains
- Behaviour:

'So, what did you do when you became anxious because of these demands and beliefs? It is often our behaviour, in such situations, that causes us difficulties,' asked Dr Bill.

'I have to admit that my cigarette and alcohol intake rocketed,' replied Hugh, 'and my exercise regime went out the window along with my sleep!'

'Any other behaviours?'

'I spent all my time living in my head, fretting constantly about how I could improve the company's financial situation and about the awful prospect of having to let my loyal staff go.'

'And did you try any behaviours other than alcohol, nicotine and ruminating to try and reduce your anxiety?'

'I spent hours and hours at night on the internet or aimlessly channel-hopping, trying to distract myself. But it never worked. I still went to bed exhausted but could not sleep so became increasingly frustrated and tired. I also spent a lot more time on my social media, which did nothing to reduce my anxiety.'

Dr Bill explained that these were quite common behaviour patterns when we become toxically stressed and they added them to their ABC:

A   Activating Event:
*   Trigger: Hugh's company getting into financial difficulties
*   Inference/Danger: He would have to let employees go to avoid the company going into administration; he would find it very difficult to fire staff to whom he had become close; the banks were making the company's situation worse; he must not have to sack his employees; he would have a very poor opinion of himself if he had to; if he does, he will feel he has failed them.

B   Belief/Demands:

C   Consequences:
*   Emotions: anxiety
*   Physical reactions: fatigue, headaches, muscle tension, weight loss, chest pains
*   Behaviour: ruminates constantly about having to let staff go; stops eating properly; sleeps poorly and stays up late at night on the internet and TV channel-hopping; constantly reduces his company's costs to avoid having to make redundancies; avoids contact with the banks; drinks and smokes too much

CHALLENGING THE A – They could challenge his inference that the company might reach a point where he would be forced by the bank to fire employees or let it go into administration, but at the moment this looked like a real possibility.

CHALLENGING THE B – Dr Bill persuades Hugh that the best approach would be to challenge the unhealthy demands he was making. He explains the concepts behind the 'Big MACS', and together they come up with the following:

MUST – First, he challenges Hugh's demand that he must not let any of his employees go. While Hugh obviously doesn't want to do this, he might have to do so.

AWFUL – He challenges Hugh's assumption that the worst would inevitably happen. He did not know how things would turn out; he was becoming stressed about a hypothetical scenario. If he did have to let employees go, it might not be as bad as he feared. He should also consider the possibility that he might be able to rehire them if the economy started to recover.

CAN'T STAND IT – He challenges Hugh's belief that he would not be able to cope if he had to let employees go. It would be in the interest of the company and the remaining employees to do so.

SELF/OTHER RATING – Finally, he challenges Hugh's statement that having to lay employees off would mean he is a failure.

CHALLENGING THE C – They decide that Hugh could not challenge his natural reactions of anxiety, or his physical symptoms, but that he could challenge his behavioural responses, in the following ways:

- Avoiding communicating with the banks was not helping.
- Discussing financial matters with advisors and accountants may be a more productive use of his time and energy.
- Smoking and drinking more was just making matters worse.
- Improving his diet, taking supplements and doing exercise would be more helpful.
- Ruminating over his difficulties was only increasing his stress.

Six months later Hugh is in a new space. He had completely revolutionized his lifestyle and was now off cigarettes, was only taking alcohol occasionally, eating healthily and even doing some meditation tapes at night before going to sleep. His late-night surfing of both the TV and internet was now a distant memory. He had also discovered the power of a good book!

But the game-changer was when he hammered out a deal with a financial advisor with his financial institution to restructure the company, which was now flying and was seriously considering hiring further staff.

His toxic stress was a distant memory!

### 'There Is No Future For Me!'

Sean is twenty-four and finds himself in a rut. He was enticed to leave school before completing his final state exam, the Leaving Cert, by the high wages being offered on the building sites. It was a great life: with his pocket full of cash, he went out with his friends every night. Once the construction industry collapsed, however, so did his world. His skills were no longer required and he could not find work; his lack of education or other skills meant that he found it impossible to secure other employment. He went back to live at home and became withdrawn and stressed. He drank to cope with his stress, his self-esteem plummeted, and he gave up applying for jobs. He started arguing with his girlfriend, and his relationship broke down. His only consolation was that most of his friends were in a similar situation. He lost weight and developed cold sores and acne, and started getting tension headaches. His mood dropped and he started to think about ending his life: like many young men under the age of twenty-five, his prospects seemed bleak.

He went out drinking with friends, who tried to lift him out of his withdrawn mood – but to no avail. Sean left the pub and headed for the river. On his way, a poster for the Samaritans caught his eye and he decided to ring the number. He found the counsellor easy to talk to, and poured out his feelings of self-loathing and hopelessness about the future. After the phone call, he felt relieved; he returned home to his parents and opened up to them. Finally, he went to see Dr Bill. After listening to Sean's story, Dr Bill realised that Sean had responded to a long period of chronic stress by becoming significantly depressed and was fortunate to have encountered the Samaritans. Dr Bill explains how stress can lead to severe depression and offers to help Sean deal with his issues. Dr Bill recommends a holistic treatment package of exercise, proper diet, supplements and antidepressants, and finally some therapy sessions. Sean agreed to stop drinking alcohol until he was feeling better. After some time, Sean began to feel better, and Dr Bill began to work with him on the issues underlying his stress and depression.

Dr Bill decides that the best way to deal with Sean's situation is to do an ABC to discover the source of his distress. He initially explains about Rational and Irrational Beliefs and how the ABC concept would work; and how they would use this system to try and locate and deal with his Irrational Beliefs.

They decide that they would use the trigger of Sean losing his job in construction.

Dr Bill begins by asking Sean, 'How did you feel emotionally when you lost your job due to the recession?'

'I just became so down,' he replied. 'I could see no hope for the future. It was a dark place!'

'And how did you feel physically when your mood dropped?'

'I was so tired all day, every day. I also found I couldn't concentrate on anything and struggled with my memory. I lost all interest in food and indeed in everything and stopped enjoying anything'.

Dr Bill explained that these physical symptoms were quite common when our mood fell and we became depressed. He asked Sean to start their ABC:

A   Activating Event:
- Trigger: Sean losing his job in construction because of the recession
- Inference/Danger:

B   Belief/Demands:

C   Consequences:
- Emotions: depression
- Physical reactions: fatigue, anorexia, reduced interest and drive, sleep difficulties and anhedonia
- Behaviour:

Dr Bill then inquired, 'What is it about your losing your job that ended up with you feeling so depressed?'

'The biggest difficulty for me was that I had left school early and did not finish my education. So, when I lost my job and was clearly unable to find another one, as the recession just wiped out the building industry, I had no-where else to turn to. It was a scary place to be at the time'.

'And how did this make you feel about yourself?'

'I just felt so useless and worthless'.

They added this to their ABC:

A   Activating Event:
- Trigger: Sean losing his job in construction because of the recession
- Inference/Danger: He could not get a different job, as he had no other skills; there was no hope of more employment in the foreseeable future; he had made a big mistake by leaving school early; there was no way out of his situation; he felt useless.

B   Belief/Demands:

C   Consequences:
- Emotions: depression
- Physical reactions: fatigue, anorexia, reduced interest and drive, sleep difficulties and anhedonia
- Behaviour:

'Let's move on to see what Irrational Belief was triggered by this situation and the inference you assigned to it' said Dr Bill. 'This usually takes the form of some absolute demand you are making about the trigger. Let's examine first what beliefs or demands were you making that resulted in you feeling so depressed'?

After some discussion, Sean decided that because he had made such bad decisions he felt that he was a total failure.

They added this to their ABC:

A   Activating Event:
- Trigger: Sean losing his job in construction because of the recession
- Inference/Danger: He could not get a different job, as he had no other skills; there was no hope of more employment in the foreseeable future; he

had made a big mistake by leaving school early; there was no way out of his situation; he felt useless.

B   Belief/Demands: Sean was a failure.

C   Consequences:
- Emotions: depression
- Physical reactions: fatigue, anorexia, reduced interest and drive, sleep difficulties and anhedonia
- Behaviour:

'So, what did you do when you became depressed because of your belief that you were a failure? It is often our behaviour, in such situations, that causes us difficulties,' asked Dr Bill.

'I found myself constantly fretting about the possibility that I might not be able to find work again. I became hopeless, withdrew into myself, cut myself off from my friends and family, began to drink more and began to seriously considering suicide as the only way he could see out of the mess I had found myself embroiled in!'

They added this to complete their ABC:

A   Activating Event:
- Trigger: Sean losing his job in construction because of the recession
- Inference/Danger: He could not get a different job, as he had no other skills; there was no hope of more employment in the foreseeable future; he had made a big mistake by leaving school early; there was no way out of his situation; he felt useless.

B   Belief/Demands: Sean was a failure.

C   Consequences:
- Emotions: depression
- Physical reactions: fatigue, anorexia, reduced interest and drive, sleep difficulties and anhedonia
- Behaviour: worries that he will not find work again; stops applying for

jobs; drinks too much and stops eating; withdraws from family and friends and considers suicide

Dr Bill then helps Sean challenge these behaviours.

CHALLENGING THE A – While they could challenge Sean's interpretation that he would not find a job in construction, or in another industry, because of his lack of schooling, this was a possibility.

CHALLENGING THE B – Dr Bill decides instead to challenge Sean's un-healthy demands and beliefs. He explains the concepts behind the 'Big MACS' but concentrates only on the rating aspect.

SELF/OTHER RATING – He challenges Sean's statement that he is a failure because he can't get work in construction.

CHALLENGING THE C – They decide that Sean has to accept his emotional reaction of depression, and his physical symptoms, as a normal reaction. Dr Bill challenges Sean's behavioural responses, however:

- Avoiding key decisions involving employment was only making matters worse.
- Going back into education to do his Leaving Cert exams, or getting additional training, would be helpful.
- Not eating, and drinking more, were not helping the situation.
- It was important for Sean to improve his diet, take supplements, and reduce his alcohol intake.
- Ruminating about his situation was not getting him anywhere.
- He could not think his way into a good situation, but he could act his way into one.

Two years later, Sean is doing much better: he has completed his Leaving Cert and is going into further education in the field of electronic engineering. He is no longer stressed and depressed, is eating well, has reduced his alcohol intake, and is exercising daily. He is in a new relationship, and is doing voluntary work for a student helpline for people his own age who have got into trouble.

The above examples show us how toxic stress can be a great threat to our mental and physical health and how, by using the 'ABC' approach and challenging our unhealthy behaviours, we can transform our lives for the better.

## Problem-solving

Before leaving this section, it would be useful to examine the concept of 'problem-solving', as this is a very useful behaviour tool when it comes to dealing with stress. Many people who suffer from chronic stress have a tendency to find themselves paralysed by indecision when it comes to choosing a course of action. This is mostly attributable to being overwhelmed by the stressor and being unable to tackle the problem in a logical manner. *This behaviour is called procrastination and can increase the difficulties created by toxic stress. It is therefore critical that we develop skills to deal with this issue.*

Here are a few helpful hints to aid problem-solving:

- Try and break down the issues facing you into smaller, more manageable problems.
- Write out these smaller problems, decide which is the most important one, and deal with that first.
- List possible ways of dealing with this problem.
- If you cannot solve this problem, take the next one on the list, and do the same thing.
- Continue until you have decided what you can and cannot do to solve each problem.
- Focus your energy on making changes where you can, and try and ignore areas over which you have little or no control.
- Approach problems one at a time.

Here are two examples of this approach in action.

## 'I Feel Overwhelmed!'

Michael is a student who has become highly stressed because he does not think he can cover all the relevant topics for an important exam. He develops all the physical and emotional symptoms of toxic stress and engages in typical unhealthy behaviours. He visits Dr Bill, and they discuss the issue. Dr Bill takes him through the problem-solving steps listed above, and they work out the following strategy for Michael to pursue:

- First, identify the main subjects where Michael already has a good grasp of the content, and summarise the main relevant points.
- Secondly, identify areas where he needs to do more work, and tackle these areas.
- List the most common topics that arise in the exams, and prepare for these based on the notes.
- Ask lecturers what they consider to me the most important areas to focus on.
- Leave the areas he finds most difficult until last.
- Do not try to cover everything, as he will be able to remember only a certain amount.
- Focus on the most important topics, so he can revise quickly before the exam.
- In the exam itself, first put down a 'skeleton' of his answer and then flesh out the details.

The main advantage of Michael taking such an approach is that it removes his biggest difficulty: the paralysed indecision which was wasting his energy. It gives him a framework within which he should study, and reduces his stress, as he is only focusing on one thing at a time. Michael applies himself in this manner and, to his surprise, passes his exam with ease!

## 'I Feel Paralysed'

Sam is forty-five and married with two children. He has been out of work for over a year, and finds himself in a rut. His wife is bringing in some funds with her part-time job, but he has exhausted himself trying to find work in the area he was trained in – as a technician.

He has become increasingly stressed with the usual toxic-stress behaviour patterns. His wife, concerned about his mental health, sends him to see Dr Bill.

They identify that his main problem is an inability to see any way out of his present situation of unemployment, and that this is going to be it for life. Dr Bill helps him to set out the following strategy:

- He should write down all the skills he possesses, in order of importance.
- He should then list off all the passions in his life – namely interests that have always grabbed his attention and which made him feel fulfilled when he was doing them.
- Then, he should research what job opportunities there are in relation to either of these two areas.
- He should see what form of upskilling he would need in order to make his skills and passions match these job opportunities.
- If he did this, it might open up a new range of opportunities for future employment and happiness.
- He should look for any relevant professional help that was available from state organisations.
- Once he had done these things, he should return to see Dr Bill.

Two years later, Sam, who had always been very musical and loved the piano, has upskilled and set up a new school to train adults and children in the basics of piano playing. His passion has become his new vocation!

Let's now examine the last and most important step in our seven-step process: how you can put all of this into action in your own life.

# STEP SEVEN
## YOUR LIFE, YOUR 'ABC'!

Tens of thousands, or perhaps even hundreds of thousands, of people in modern Ireland and in other parts of the developed and developing world are experiencing chronic stress. Many more are in danger of developing chronic stress, but may not fully appreciate the risks. You or someone close to you may be experiencing it. Let's outline the steps necessary to deal with stress. This process will target your particular problems, so you must be honest with yourself when it comes to analysing your particular situation and how it is affecting you.

## Step One

You need to learn how to recognise whether or not chronic stress is actually a problem in your life. Physical symptoms are usually more immediately obvious than emotional ones. It takes real courage to face the unhealthy behaviours that accompany these symptoms, however. Here, I will outline these symptoms and behaviours again, so that you can review them and decide which relate to you. It should then become clear how chronic stress is affecting your life.

### Physical Symptoms
- exhaustion
- sleep difficulties, including waking up early, grinding teeth and having nightmares
- tension headaches, often chronic

- abdominal upset, stomach cramps
- sweating, palpitations, chronic sighing and difficulty breathing
- muscle tension and pains
- bouts of viral and bacterial illnesses, including cold sores and mouth ulcers
- loss of libido
- obesity or weight loss
- restlessness, poor concentration, and difficulty finishing tasks
- poor short-term memory

## Psychological Symptoms
- frustration, anger and intolerance, which are characteristic of those in the high-risk group
- panic attacks and worrying
- a sense of hopelessness
- depression, negative thinking, feelings of worthlessness, and suicidal thoughts
- fixed and immutable thinking, creating conflict at home and at work
- inability to make decisions, or poor judgement
- addiction

## Unhealthy Behaviours
- increase in smoking and alcohol consumption
- a tendency to stop exercising
- eating poorly
- misusing stimulants such as caffeine or energy drinks
- taking illegal drugs such as hash or cocaine
- addiction to prescription medication, such as tranquillizers, to ease anxiety

Having identified that there is a problem, your next step involves ruling out physical and psychological illnesses which may offer an alternative explanation for your symptoms. This will require a visit to your family doctor. Such conditions include anaemia, diabetes, thyroid disease and depression.

There are two other important questions you need to ask as part of this assessment:

1. What is my family history? Is there a history of heart disease, blood pressure, diabetes, depression, addiction or anxiety?
2. Do I seem to be exhibiting any of the personality traits outlined earlier? These might predispose me a greater possibility of stress-related illnesses.

Your family history or personality may provide insight into the source of your problems and the risks you face. If a person fits into the type A personality and has a strong family history of angina or heart attacks, they are particularly at risk of experiencing serious problems if they develop chronic stress.

The next key step is to examine your lifestyle to see if any of the above unhealthy behaviours are present. Regardless of the stressor and its physical and emotional impact on an individual, these behaviours will only make the problem worse. Behaviours such as smoking, drinking, eating junk food and misusing drugs may provide short-term relief but are damaging to the person's health in the long term. If we are not prepared to change these behaviours, we remain at high risk of developing serious problems as a result of chronic stress. Other alternative therapies, such as meditation, mindfulness, yoga and pilates, can be helpful, and nutritional supplements can also reduce the negative effects of stress. Once you have identified the unhealthy behaviours relevant to you, you need to make the appropriate lifestyle changes.

Step one can be the most difficult, as it involves becoming attuned to our physical and emotional state, and being honest with ourselves regarding our lifestyle. It is worth mentioning here the significant differences between men and women in relation to how the two sexes tend to deal with this step. Men may find it more difficult to verbalise their emotions, and as a result will use a catch-all term such as 'stress', whereas women will admit to being anxious, depressed or frustrated. Men generally avoid doctors unless they are in real difficulty, and may see it as a sign of weakness in themselves to be complaining of the above symptoms. Men can also be difficult to diagnose: for example, the latest research suggests that many men with significant depression actually present with outbursts of anger.

## Step Two

The next step involves writing down the stressors which we believe underly the above symptoms and behaviours. These may be related to exams, financial difficulties, relationship problems, health, sexual-identity issues, unemployment, bullying, abuse or addiction. We then need to rank the stressors in order of significance and decide which one to deal with first. You should then take the stressor in question and do an 'ABC' analysis on it, as follows:

- Take a page and divide it up into three areas, designating them as 'A', 'B' and 'C'.
- Under 'A', write 'Trigger', and under that 'Inference/Danger'.
- Under 'B', write 'Demands/Beliefs'.
- Under 'C', write 'Consequences', and under that 'Emotions', 'Physical Symptoms' and 'Behaviours'.

**A**

Trigger

Inference/Danger

**B**

Beliefs/Demands

**C**

Consequences

Emotions

Physical Symptoms

Behaviours

We now have a simple tool to analyse exactly why a particular stressor is causing us trouble in our lives.

## 'I May Be Made Redundant!'

Mary has completed step one, recognised the symptoms of chronic stress in her life, and eliminated other possibilities. She has listed five main stressors and decided that her major one is the fear that she may be made redundant.

Here is how she would approach the problem:

A   Activating Event:
- Trigger: rumours that there is due to be a meeting on the following Friday in relation to 'restructuring' the company
- Inference/Danger: Mary would ask herself the key question, 'Why is this bothering me?' and fill in the answer roughly as follows: If they are holding such a meeting, they may be going to lay off staff, and I might be one of those offered redundancy; I would then struggle, as my husband is already working part-time, and we have a significant mortgage on the house, which we would struggle to pay; we would get into difficulties with the bank and may end up having to fight to keep the house; I couldn't cope with losing the house after all the work and money we have invested in it; I would be letting my children down, as we would struggle to pay for many of the activities they enjoy.

B   Belief/Demands: Here, Mary identifies the key unhealthy beliefs and demands that are leading her to be so distressed: She must not be let go from her job; If she is let go, she will be unable to cope with the consequences; If she is let go, she will be a failure.

C   Consequences:
- Emotions: Mary identifies how she feels as a consequence of her unhealthy demand above, and writes down 'anxiety' and 'low mood'.
- Physical reactions: She identifies the physical symptoms she is experiencing as a result of her anxiety and low mood, and writes down 'fatigue', 'headaches', 'muscle tension' and 'stomach upset'.

- Behaviour: She identifies the unhealthy behaviours which have become a response to her emotional and physical symptoms above. She notes that she: ruminates constantly on the fear of losing her job; tries excessively hard to do her work perfectly; becomes irritable with work colleagues due to exhaustion and frustration; is sleeping poorly; eats junk food; smokes more cigarettes than before; drinks more alcohol than before; stops exercising.

## Step Three

Now that she has outlined the problem, the next task is to examine the trigger and ask why it is bothering her. While it is sometimes obvious why an event would cause significant stress, an inaccurate interpretation of an event can also cause problems. In either case, we must evaluate the stressor in order to understand why it is a problem for us.

Let's recap on Mary's trigger, and her interpretation of it:

TRIGGER: Rumours that there is due to be a meeting the following Friday in relation to 'restructuring' the company.

Mary should then write down the evidence for her interpretation. What proof does she have that she will be laid off? While it is not beyond the realms of possibility, it is not certain to happen either. Furthermore, even if she is laid off, she has plenty of options open to her to avoid losing the family home. She also has no proof that she will end up letting her children down, or that they will be unhappy because the family is now on a tighter budget. While it is useful to challenge the 'A' in this instance, it is more helpful to challenge the demands and beliefs she places on herself.

## Step Four

Here we move on to challenge our unhealthy beliefs and demands arising from our interpretation of our stressor. Let's take Mary's demands again:

B   Belief/Demands: She must not be let go from her job; if she is let go, she will be unable to cope with the consequences; if she is let go, she will be a failure.

She has made one unhealthy demand: that she must not be let go from her job. She has also stated two unhealthy beliefs: that she will not be able to cope with the consequences and that if she loses her job she will be a failure. We can now use the 'Big MACS' to help her challenge these three unhealthy demands and beliefs.

MUST – It seems as if Mary is living in the land of 'must', which involves an absolute demand which is usually impossible to deliver. It would be healthier to use the word 'prefer', as it is more realistic. It would of course be preferable to not lose her job – but there are many things outside of Mary's control, such as the economic climate. She is demanding complete certainty that she will not lose her job, and this is not possible.

AWFUL – Mary should challenge her assumption that the worst would inevitably happen. She is visualising that her family will be out on the streets, but this scenario is unlikely to happen.

CAN'T STAND IT – She believes that, if the worst did occur, she would be unable to cope. In fact, although things would be very difficult, she would almost certainly get through it for the sake of her family.

SELF/OTHER RATING – Finally, she should challenge her statement that she would be a failure if she lost her job.

## Step Five

Here, we move on to evaluate the emotional, physical and behavioural consequences of the unhealthy demands and beliefs we hold in response to stressors. Lets have another look at Mary's 'consequences' and see how she can challenge them.

EMOTIONS: Mary identifies how she feels as a consequence of her unhealthy demand above, and writes down 'anxiety' and 'low mood'.

PHYSICAL REACTIONS: She identifies the physical symptoms she is experiencing as a result of the emotions of anxiety and low mood, and writes down 'fatigue', 'headaches', 'muscle tension' and 'stomach upset'.

BEHAVIOUR: Mary identifies the unhealthy behaviours which are a response to the emotions and physical symptoms outlined above, and writes them down.

It is of little help to challenge her emotional or physical responses, but it is useful to list them in order to help Mary understand how her demands and beliefs are affecting her. Mary should challenge her unhealthy behaviours as follows:

- Ruminating constantly is not helping resolve the problem.
- Being irritable with colleagues at work is not likely to increase her chances of keeping her job.
- Eating poorly, not exercising, and smoking and drinking to excess are only making her feel worse.

Mary could reduce the negative effects of toxic stress if she began to make changes along these lines. Lifestyle changes such as doing more exercise, eating properly, taking supplements, doing yoga or pilates, or going to mindfulness classes would help her greatly.

## Step Six

This is where we put everything together:

- Mary has realised that she is experiencing toxic stress, after eliminating any other physical and psychological causes for the way she is feeling.
- She listed her main stressors and placed them in order of significance, and

chose the one she feels is the most problematic.

- She did an 'ABC' of her problem.
- She challenged the stress trigger and analysed why it was bothering her.
- She challenged her unhealthy beliefs/demands.
- Finally, she challenged her unhealthy behaviours and resolved to change them.
- She put all these things together to create a picture of why the stressor is causing her so much difficulty and how she can deal with it most effectively.

At the end of this process, Mary has a much better idea of what is causing her problems with stress, how it is affecting her and, most importantly, how to change her thinking and behaviour in order to reduce the risks toxic stress poses to her.

To summarise our seven steps:

1. What is the main cause of toxic stress in your life?
2. What are your thoughts/emotions and behaviour in relation to the stressor? ('ABC')
3. Is your interpretation of the stressor valid?
4. What unhealthy beliefs/demands are you making?
5. What are the behavioural consequences of your unhealthy beliefs?
6. Develop a working 'ABC' model.
7. Remember: *this is your life!*

Some readers will quickly grasp these steps and put them into practice in their lives, while others may seek expert help (and certainly should not be afraid of doing so!). Most of us have the capacity to handle these concepts ourselves; we just need a framework to work within. I have been amazed, from the feedback from readers of my previous books, by how quickly people in distress were able to grasp key ideas and put them into practice in their lives; dealing with stress is no different. Most of us need just three things in order to deal with stress in our lives:

- knowledge
- a simple, structured framework for dealing with the problem
- persistence

To tackle stress, we need to be:

- self-observant of the symptoms and emotions arising from toxic stress
- brutally honest with ourselves in our assessment of the stressors and how we are choosing to interpret them
- brave enough to identify and challenge the key unhealthy demands and beliefs we hold
- strong enough to challenge the resulting unhealthy behavioural consequences

The prize is invaluable: preventing chronic, toxic stress from wreaking physical and emotional havoc in your life. Your survival may depend upon it. The choice is yours!

# BIBLIOGRAPHY

Akil, H. (2005). 'Stressed and depressed'. *Nature Medicine*, 11, 116-118

Barry, H. P. (2009). *Flagging the Therapy: Pathways out of Depression and Anxiety*. Dublin: Liberties Press

---.(2007). *Flagging the Problem: A New Approach to Mental Health*. Dublin: Liberties Press

Bangasser. D. A. (2016). 'Stress' *Scientific American Mind* 27, 58–63

Brosan, L. and G. Todd (2007). *Overcoming Stress*. London: Robinson

Canli, T. and K. P. Lesch (2007), 'Long story short: the serotonin transporter in emotion regulation and social cognition', *Nature Neuroscience*, 10 (9), 1103-9

Charney, D. S. & H. K. Manji (2004). 'Life stress, genes, and depression: Multiple pathways lead to increased risk and new opportunities for intervention'. *Science Signalling*, 225, 5

Dishman, R. K. et al (2006). 'Neurobiology of exercise'. *Obesity*, 14, 345-56

Doidge, N. (2008). *The Brain That Changes Itself*. London: Penguin Books

Ellis, A. and R. A. Harper (1975). *A Guide to Rational Living*. California: Wilshere Book Company.

Harrison, E. (2003). *The 5 Minute Meditator*. London: Piatkus Kabat-Zinn, J. (2008). *Wherever You Go, There You Are*. London: Piatkus

Kabat-Zinn, J. (2008). *Full Catastrophe Living*. London: Piatkus

Looker, T. and O. Gregson (2003). *Teach Yourself: Managing Stress*. London: Hodder Education

Meaney, M.J. (2001). Maternal care, gene expression, and the transmission of individual differences in stress reactivity  across generations Annual Rev

Neuroscience 24:1161-92.

Murphy, E. (2009). 'The raggy doll club'. *Forum, Journal of the Irish College of General Practitioners*

Palmer, S. and C. Cooper (2007). *How to Deal with Stress*. London: Kogan Page

Russo-Neustadt, A. A., R. C. Beard, Y. M. Huang and C. W. Cotman (2000), 'Physical activity and antidepressant treatment potentiate the expression of specific brain-derived neurotrophic factor transcripts in the rat hippocampus', Neuroscience, 101 (2), 305-12

Sapolsky, R. (2003). 'Taming stress'. *Scientific American*, (2003)

Williams, M. et al (2007). *The Mindful Way through Depression*. New York: the Guildford Press

# HELP AND SUPPORT

## Alcoholics Anonymous

Alcoholics Anonymous 'AA' is an international organisation with over 2,000,000 members who have recovered or are suffering from alcohol abuse or addiction. AA is concerned solely with the personal recovery and continued sobriety of individual alcoholics; it does not engage in the fields of alcoholism research, medical or psychiatric treatment, education, or advocacy in any form but provides peer-to-peer support within a Fellowship structure. There are approximately 4,400 group meetings each week throughout Great Britain. The AA is fully self-supporting and does not accept donations from non-members. All contributions are voluntary.

Helpline: 0800 917 7650

help@aamail.org | www.alcoholics-anonymous.org.uk

## Anxiety UK

Anxiety UK is a national registered charity formed in 1970 to provide help for anyone affected by anxiety, stress and anxiety-based depression. The website maintains an up-to-date list of independent, verified self-help groups located across the UK and provides a wealth of self help resources online.

Helpline: 08444 755 744

support@anxietyuk.org.uk | www.anxietyuk.org.uk

## Aware

Aware is a voluntary organisation established in 1985 to support those experiencing depression and their families. Aware endeavours to create a society where people with mood disorders and their families are understood and supported, and able to obtain the resources to enable them to defeat depression. Weekly support group meetings at approximately fifty locations nationwide, including Northern Ireland, offer peer support, provide factual information, and enable people to gain the skills they need to help them cope with depression. Aware's 'Beat the Blues' educational programme is run in secondary schools.

Helpline: 1890 303 302 (Ireland only)
support@aware.ie | www.aware.ie | 01 661 7211

## ChildLine

ChildLine, a service run by the NSPCC, seeks to empower and support children using the medium of telecommunications and information technology. The service is designed for all children and young people up to the age of eighteen in Ireland.

Helpline: 0800 1111

## Grow

Established in Ireland in 1969, GROW is Ireland's largest mutual-help organisation in the area of mental health. It is anonymous, nondenominational, confidential and free. No referrals are necessary. GROW aims to achieve self-activation through mutual help. Its members are enabled, over time, to craft a step-by-step recovery or personal-growth plan, and to develop leadership skills that will help others.

Helpline: 1 890 474 474 (Ireland only)
info@grow.ie | www.grow.ie

# Mind

Mind is one of the UK's leading mental health charities. The organisation has been committed to making sure that mental health advice and support is accessible for anyone who needs it. In 2013 the charity successfully campaigned against the Mental Health (Discrimination) Act, removing the last significant forms of discrimination that prevented people with mental health problems from serving on a jury, being a director of a company or serving as an MP. With over 375,000 local Minds across England and Wales, the charity provides millions with services that include supported housing, crisis helplines, drop-in centres, employment and training schemes, counselling, peer support, information and befriending.

Helpline: 0300 123 3393
info@mind.org.uk | www.mind.org.uk

# No Panic

No Panic is a charity which aims to facilitate the relief and rehabilitation of people suffering from panic attacks, phobias, obsessive compulsive disorders and other related anxiety disorders, including tranquilliser withdrawal, and to provide support to sufferers and their families and carers. Founded by Colin M. Hammond in the UK, this group has extended its activities to Ireland, where it is organised by therapist Caroline McGuigan.

Helpline: 0844 967 4848
Youth Helpline: 0175 384 0393
admin@nopanic.org.uk | nopanic.org.uk | 0195 268 0460

## Samaritans

Samaritans was started in 1953 in London by a young vicar called Chad Varah; the first branch in the Republic of Ireland opened in Dublin in 1970. Samaritans provides a twenty-four-hour-a-day confidential service offering emotional support for people who are experiencing feelings of distress or despair, including those which may lead to suicide.

Helpline: 116 123
jo@samaritans.org | www.samaritans.org

## Sane

Established in 1986 to improve the quality of life for all those affected by mental health problems, SANE is a UK-wide charity with three main objectives: to raise awareness and combat stigma about mental illness; to provide emotional support and care; to aid research into the causes and treatments of serious mental health conditions such as schizophrenia and depression. SANE provides confidential emotional support, information and access to self-management strategies.

Helpline: 0300 304 7000
info@sane.org.uk | www.sane.org.uk

# ACKNOWLEDGEMENTS

I would like to start by thanking my editorial team at Orion for all their wonderful assistance in republishing this book. In particular, I want to thank Olivia Morris who has believed in the *Flag* series from the beginning and who has been so supportive. I also owe a huge debt of gratitude to Vanessa Fox O'Loughlin and Dominic Perrim my two agents who have made all of this possible.

I must particularly mention my friend and colleague Enda Murphy and his invaluable assistance.

There are a number of people who sadly will not be here to see this published. The first is my brother David. We still miss you. The second is our great family friend Sister Kieran Saunders MMM, who is mentioned in my last book. We miss you so much Kieran, and pray that you will remain our 'spiritual guide' throughout this mysterious journey through the pathways of life and beyond. Finally my mother, Dilly Barry (Thurles), who has lost her long battle with illness (which she had faced with bravery and courage),

As always, I reserve my biggest 'thank you' to my wife Brenda, whose love, friendship, support, encouragement, and particularly patience has made this book and indeed the whole series possible. You are my light in the darkness, and truly my soulmate. '*Mo ghra, mo chroi.*' (My love, my heart).

A practical guide to understanding, managing
and overcoming anxiety and panic attacks.

ANXIETY
AND PANIC

How to reshape your
anxious mind and brain

DR HARRY BARRY

A practical, four step programme to help you
understand and cope with depression.

DEPRESSION

A practical guide

DR HARRY BARRY

A practical guide to understanding and coping with anxiety, depression, addiction and suicide.

FLAGGING THE
PROBLEM

A new approach to
mental health

DR HARRY BARRY

S

A practical guide exploring the role of therapy in depression and anxiety.

FLAGGING THE
THERAPY

Pathways out of
depression and anxiety

DR HARRY BARRY

S